Living on
Less
and
Liking it
More

OTHER BOOKS BY MAXINE HANCOCK:

Can I Really Have it All? (NavPress, 1991; reprint, Regent College Publishing, 1999.)

Child Sexual Abuse: A Hope for Healing. Co-author, Karen Burton Mains. (Harold Shaw Publishers, 1987; rev. ed., 1997).

Creative, Confident Children. (Revell, 1978; 1st rev. ed., Harold Shaw Publishers, 1991; 2nd rev. ed., Regent College Publishing, 2001).

Love Knows no Difference: Learning to Give and Receive. (Harvest House, 1983; reprint, Regent College Publishing, 1999).

Re-Evaluating Your Commitments. (First published as *The Forever Principle.* Revell, 1980; rev. ed. Bethany House, 1990; reprint, Regent College Publishing, 2001).

ACADEMIC:

The Key in the Window: Marginal Notes in Bunyan's Narratives. (Regent College Publishing, 2000).

Readings in Biblical Hebrew: An Intermediate Textbook. Co-authors, Ehud Ben-Zvi and Richard Beinert (Yale University Press, 1993).

Maxine Hancock

Living on Less and Liking it More

how to reduce your spending and increase your living

Regent College Publishing • Vancouver

National Library of Canada Cataloguing in Publication Data

Hancock, Maxine.
  Living on less and liking it more : how to reduce your spending and
increase your living / Maxine Hancock.

  Includes bibliographical references and index.
  ISBN 1-55361-062-8 (Canada)
  ISBN 1-57383-138-7 (United States)

  1. Christian life. 2. Materialism—Religious aspects—Christianity.
3. Values. 4. Cost and standard of living. I. Title.

BV4501.2.H32 2002   241'.68   C2002-911235-4

To
my parents,
MAX and RUTH RUNIONS,
who have known and shown
that
"godliness with contentment is
great gain"

CONTENTS

First, This Word

"When times are good, be happy; but when times are bad, consider" (Ecc. 7:14).

I did not set out to write a book in praise of poverty, for I find little about poverty to celebrate. I like the honesty of Samuel Johnson who is reported to have said, "While I was running about this town a very poor fellow, I was a great arguer for the advantages of poverty; but I was, at the same time, very sorry to be poor."

All the nostalgic reviving in books and television of the "good old days" when money was scarce but love was plentiful, all the romanticizing of the "pastoral dream" in which folks more or less effortlessly live off the land, leave me very unmoved. For nothing can blot out the fact that poverty is a sharply painful experience. I will have to leave to others the task of writing happy memoirs about the joys of voluntary poverty. We have had a taste of hardship — not that we exactly volunteered for it — and I consider poverty a state to be avoided. I can think of no more appropriate prayer for each other than that recorded by the loving Apostle John, "Dear friend, I pray that you may enjoy good health and that all may go well with you, even as your soul is getting along well" (3 John 2).

Nevertheless, my husband Cam and I did find "the day of adversity" to be a good time to consider and reconsider almost everything. And we have lived the many years since that time in the light of what we learned. Through a jolting business reversal, we came to an understanding of the problems of poverty and the joys of modest living. And we found that modest — and even meager — living could be a way of learning to re-examine our values and of learning to grow in love.

As young teachers, fresh out of university at a time when teachers were in great demand, we had enjoyed the comfort of regular and adequate wages. And then we decided to go farming. I still gulp hard when I type that and remember how, beginning with nothing, we set out to borrow the large amount of money necessary to begin a farming operation. Those first few years were rough. But we did manage to make our mortgage payments and meet basic needs — not only for ourselves, but for a family to which we were just then adding a new baby every couple of years.

And then, just as we were beginning to feel that we were getting on our feet financially, we saw an opportunity that was too good to miss. Forming a limited company with another couple, we operated a joint grain-growing and cattle-feeding operation. For three years our grain crops were fed through cattle. On paper, the plan looked foolproof, of course. But just as the loans we had taken to launch this larger enterprise began to mature and demand repayment, the cattle market slid into a deep depression. We had to sell our fattened beef animals at prices far below production costs. And when we awakened one August morning to find that we had also lost our entire crop to an unseasonably early frost, we ground to the sudden halt of insolvency. It was a terrible, frantic, lost, hopeless feeling—one that has become all too familiar in more recent years to many people in North America, as apparently sure jobs have vanished in corporate downsizing, and seemingly invincible enterprises have faltered.

Looking back now, we wonder if we would have kept what sanity we salvaged, had we not been able to laugh. We had a kind of black humor that helped us through—lines like, "Well, one thing's for sure, when the big depression hits, we're going to have had years of practice," or Cam's, "I just wish I'd listened to my folks and gone to university—then I could have been somewhere warm, wearing a tie." There was, of course, financial uncertainty built into both of our vocations, my writing and Cam's farming.

Through all those hard days, we learned . . . so much.

The reflections of this book were originally written "the morning after" the day of adversity. I wanted to share what we had learned—new values and attitudes toward life. But I am coming back to this book for yet another edition in quite different circumstances. When our children were in post-secondary training, we cinched in our belts again so I could return to graduate studies. For several years after I completed doctoral studies, we continued to spend our summers on the farm and our winters in a city where I could teach and write. During those years, Cam was involved in farm organizations and agricultural practices promoting soil conservation and ecologically responsible agriculture. Finally, Cam leased out our farmland, and I turned my attention to full-time teaching at Regent College in Vancouver, Canada, where I now teach Inter-disciplinary Studies and Spiritual Theology. Should I perhaps be writing a sequel, rather than a new edition? Maybe something really saleable, like *Living on More and Liking it Better?*

I remember a day when I walked down a country road into a biting winter wind and argued with myself about whether I should even finish the manuscript for the first edition. By the time I had finished writing it, we had extricated ourselves from the most acute stage of the financial collapse we had experienced; we had found off-farm jobs, income was beginning to trickle in from my writing, and I thought: why not just chuck it, and live out to the edges of whatever prosperity the Lord might bless us with? Because writing the book and publishing it was a kind of commitment, a binding of ourselves to live by those values we had bruised ourselves in learning, to carry forward into the rest of our life our sense of God's call to modest living, regardless of our means.

Now, nearly two decades after the first publication of this book, many of our younger friends are asking tough questions about what a Christian lifestyle should look like. Questions like:

- Shouldn't Christian values de-materialize our lives?
- How do we learn to say, 'Enough's enough'? And at what point should we be saying it?
- Isn't there more to life than an endless scramble for money and things? Isn't there some way we can learn again how to really live?
- How will we face Christ our Lord and Judge if we have lived selfishly in a hungry, needy world?

This book is for these young people — now young people who are trying to figure out how to measure their lives qualitatively rather than only quantitatively; young people who are evaluating their lives in the light of a renewed sense of responsibility to others.

The first edition of the book came out along with several other books that have raised our consciousness concerning global and personal responsibility: Doris Janzen Longacre's *More-With-Less Cookbook* (Herald Press, 1976) and Ronald Sider's *Rich Christians in an Age of Hunger* (InterVarsity Press, 1977) also brought practical and theological perspectives to the discussion of evaluating our accepted North American affluence. Some of my own thinking was touched off not only by our own circumstances but by Sherwood Wirt's *The Social Conscience of the Evangelical* (Harper and Row, 1968) and W. Stanley Mooneyham's *What Do You Say to a Hungry World?*

(Word, 1975). All of us began to take a second look at our kitchen counters and our grocery carts. Later books would continue the discussion of which this book is a part. Born in my own need to evaluate attitudes and habits in the face of economic hardship, it presses on to ask questions I am still working on answering: How do we respond to the poor who are always with us? How do we react when we ourselves are the poor? And when we're not? We are realizing that our choices as consumers do affect others' lives; that we are, as I believer, in this global village, our "brothers' and sisters' keepers" with a responsibility for the well-being of others as well as of our own selves and our families. We are all uneasily aware that deep changes in patterns of production and distribution have become essential. And so the discussion of this book continues to be timely.

I am writing out of our lives for those who are hurting financially; for those who are hurting in conscience, uneasily questioning their values and trying to find guidelines for a Christian lifestyle; and for Cam and me and for our children — all now twenty-somethings, launching themselves in diverse careers at a difficult time. What this book is about is *modest living*, about learning to live at a somewhat lower standard than what we have come to accept as the norm, about finding a balance point between poverty and riches where we can live in love to our Lord, to our families, to our world.

I write as a Christian, committed to living out my life under the Lordship of Jesus Christ, and according to the principles of the Bible, through which He continues to speak to me. What I have to say, however, may well be of interest to others who, while not sharing my religious convictions, find themselves in modest or even extreme circumstances. Whether they have come to be in such circumstances by the front door of idealistic choice or the back door of necessity, there are many who want to engage in the process of understanding a set of values that puts things in their place.

I invite you to join us on our journey toward life lived joyfully and, at least on our best days, not entirely selfishly.

ACKNOWLEDGMENTS

In preparing this book for this new edition, I continue to accrue debts of appreciation to people who have been generous with their time and wisdom. I consulted with Deanna Swinamer, a dietician and family physician who helped me with the revisions to chapter 7; University of Alberta Professor Bruce Wilkinson, international economist, and Greg Brandenbarg, international justice educator, who gave me their perspectives on the larger ecnomic issues facing us today; Lyle Larson, University of Alberta professor and family sociologist, who helped me with materials and resources and an ongoing conversation about the contemporary family.

In preparing earlier editions of this book, I was helped by editors Les Stobbe of Moody Press and James R. Adair of Victor Books. For this new edition, Rob Clements of Regent College Publishing has been unfailingly helpful: my thanks go to these, and to all who have believed in this book and its message enough to encourage me to present it again to a new readership.

And always, to Cam, who walks with me; to a circle of friends who encourage me; and to my students at Regent College who continuously challenge me, my continuing grateful thanks.

—Maxine Hancock
Regent College, 2002

Chapter One

The Call to
Modest Living

It was Abe's illness that called Abe and Carole out of their comfort zone to work together in new ways and learn to trust God for things which they formerly had pretty much taken for granted.

The day I went to see them, they were enjoying the warmth and comfort of a new living-room rug, a Christmas gift from a member of their family. But the clean, neat room was sparsely furnished, and hard times were in evidence. Abe was still getting used to being blind, a result of hemorrhaging caused by diabetes. "It's not black," he explained. "It's just gray." But he couldn't see anything, not even the pretty faces of his little girls rapidly turning into young ladies, nor the face of his wonderful wife, Carole.

I sat there with them, trying to "sit where they sat," trying to imagine how we would react to such a problem. "Didn't you protest? Rebel? Cry out, 'Why me, God?' " I asked.

Abe shook his head. "God is God," he said simply. "And," he added, "I had a good model to follow when tough times came. We grew up in the dried-out prairies. I can remember years when there was no crop at all. But my folks used to plant potatoes in the slough beds, the only place where there might possibly be enough moisture to grow anything. And I can remember going out with my father to dig potatoes in the fall, and watching him stand there in that slough bottom and stop to thank God for the potatoes, for food for his family during the winter ahead. So I guess I learned early to accept and to trust."

And Carole explained, "I think it was harder for me to accept Abe's blindness than it was for Abe himself. He was really amazing. He just accepted that if this was his lot, he would have to learn to live with it."

They told me, together, of how they had learned lessons in the recent months of financial hardship that they had missed in the earlier years of their married lives.

"Like what?" I asked.

"Like the faithfulness of God. Everything we had ever believed was put to the test, and God is just as good as His Word declares Him to be. Time after time, we would have used our last dollar, and not have any idea where to turn, when the Lord would supply. Once it was by a letter in the mail. Another time — a Sunday morning — a friend pressed a gift of money into our hands when he shook hands with us at the end of the service."

"We learned, too," Abe told me, "how little material things really matter. Before I was blind, things mattered to me. A lot. Like, what kind of car I had, or my clothes." I had looked at the picture on the piano of a big, handsome Abe with Carole, his young bride, beside him. That other Abe, that Abe "before the darkness," had been a hard-working, self-reliant, things-oriented man, he told me. "But now," Abe said, "the only real things are the things of the spirit. I have learned to really *see* in another realm." He was thoughtful for a moment. "And it has made me appreciate my wife more than ever before."

To Abe and Carole — despite all of the financial problems, all the personal readjustments as Carole shouldered wage earning and Abe took up household tasks — the experience was summed up: "To us, this is not a tragedy but an opportunity." They have found in adversity an opportunity to really get to know God, an opportunity to reevaluate things, a new kind of opportunity for service.

Many people, like Abe and Carole, have had to face the economic results of severe illness or disability—a car accident, a kidney failure, a stroke, a heart attack. With the lost earning power come the often overwhelming medical expenses. Such circumstances may force the family to drastically revise its standard of living—sometimes permanently.

Others have had seemingly secure jobs wrenched from them by conditions beyond their control. During the past few years many people who had previously felt secure in their ability to earn a living have been forced into the emotional turmoil and economic difficulties accompanying job loss. Not the statistics in *Time* but the happy relief in my friend's voice as she told me, "We're happy—at least Tom still has work and can put the bread on the table—" tells the real tale of the threat of unemployment.

When the breadwinner (or breadwinners) of a family are out of work for even a few weeks or months, the call to modest living cannot be avoided. Many, having lost professional or skilled work, have to accept lower-paying jobs. And the standard of living must, often painfully, be adjusted to the new economic facts of the family's existence.

For others, retirement from the work force brings about an enforced revision—one that is often acutely painful—of their lifestyle. Many people now entering retirement experienced struggle during the early part of their earning years. Remembering the hard and lean years, they feel sharp anxiety at having once again, in old age and failing health, to suffer the effects of economic deprivation.

Others are hearing a less strident but just as unavoidable call to more modest living. For various reasons, many young people are considering seriously a call to a simple lifestyle. It is a way of freeing themselves from a materialistically motivated "rat race" in which some feel trapped; a way of living for values other than things; a way of conserving the limited resources of our small earth; or a way of making more money from their incomes available for sharing with those in need.

Annabelle and Ron, for instance, have been married for

about six years, enjoying the "Double-Income, No Kids" stage of life. Now Annabelle has left her university teaching career and is staying at home with their first child, excitedly learning about "child development" (along with "mother development") at close range. Ron is asking himself some hard questions about whether it is worth his while to cling to the high rung of the corporate ladder that he has reached. He has excellent wages as well as opportunities for travel and continuing education with the company for which he works. But his job absorbs his time and energy almost completely. And the company requires that he move periodically from one big city to another, in order to take increasingly responsible jobs.

"There's got to be more to life than this," he says thoughtfully. "I want to supply my family with more than just things. I want to share in their growing up, deeply and intimately." Right now it is just a dream, but Annabelle and Ron are thinking seriously about finding a way to work only part-time each and live modestly on a lower shared wage so that together they can enjoy more of the tasks of being parents.

Other young people have set the example. Twenty-five years ago, Will left a government job. He and his wife, Marion, each worked limited part-time hours — she at teaching nursing; he, as an economic consultant — to create a modest, pooled "living allowance." The rest of their energy went into creating a simple lifestyle on a small farm. Both having grown up in the country, they knew what they were doing and what sacrifices were required. "We can live together as a family this way," they said. "The children can know the joy of finding new kittens in the loft, and we can share that joy with them." The children have grown — and treasure the values Will and Marion passed on to them.

A Call to Modest Living

Thus, a new appreciation of the real needs of families is creating a call to more modest living for some. Another growing realization that is forcing itself upon our thinking is that the luxurious lifestyle which has been so generally adopted is, in large measure, responsible for the ecological problems we now face. Francis Schaeffer sees "hurry and greed" as the dual cause of most ecological damage:

> *Almost always,* the scar and the ugliness are the results of hurry. And whether it is hurry or greed, these things eat away at nature. But as Christians we have to learn to say "Stop!" Because . . . greed is destructive against nature at this point and there is a time to take one's time.[1]

With this awareness, many young people are altering their lifestyles, attempting to reduce their own personal consumption of the earth's resources.

Then, too, some young people are taking steps to live on less than what they earn in order that they might have more to share. In a Midwestern city, a doctor and his wife sold their large home in an exclusive district and relocated to a modest house in a working-man's section of the same city. They choose to drive a plain and aging car. They grow a garden. Now, with an income much larger than their reduced family needs, they are able to give generously to missions, world relief, and their local church. To them, the call of Jesus Christ was to a more modest lifestyle. They heard and responded with obedience.

While not all believers are being called to take such drastic action to change their lifestyles, many are looking for ways to trim the budget, to be more conservative in their spending, and thus, either to reduce their personal needs in order to live comfortably on a lower income, leaving them more time and energy for other pursuits compatible with their Christian commitment, or to leave themselves a wider margin of income over needs, from which they can share more bountifully with others.

The fact is that the Christian church in North America, which had become bogged down in the things-based value system which until recently dominated Western culture, is — slowly —

awakening to other values. More and more, Christians are becoming uncomfortably aware that some of the very basic principles of Christianity were sold or traded cheaply at a garage sale of values in mid-century. We are struggling back toward an emphasis on such things as love, compassion, and sharing.

The failure of a number of innovative communal living experiments formed during the rush of idealism in the late 1960s and 1970s should not blind us to the importance of having a range of models for the economic setup of homes and families. Intentional communities of various kinds, where people pool their resources in order to free some or all of the members for commitments to prayer or action — or both — continue to exist and to play their part in reminding us that we need to "be on [our] guard against all kinds of greed; a [person's] life does not consist in the abundance of his [or her] possessions" (Luke 12:15). And while the family is still the most functional basic economic cooperative, there are all kinds of variations on the traditional roles within the nuclear family which are reminding us that families have only recently become as isolated and nuclear as they now are.

When I was in the stage of grieving my empty nest, a woman came up to me after a conference session in which I had spoken and took my hand. "Don't be too sad," she said. "Nowadays, children come back!" Her words proved to be prophetic: Several years later, when our eldest son's wife left him with two preschool daughters, he and his little girls came "home to the farm." Since Geoff is a pilot who flies water-bombers in the Canadian north on a summer contract, we spend the summers at the farm not just farming, but also looking after two darling granddaughters. And now, our quite unintentional community also includes a sister whose marriage, after thirty-four years, has ended. In fact, we live like some sort of ancient tribe, with grandparents and great-aunts and motherless children all sharing one roof, dividing up the work and childcare and creating a safe and loving space for healing.

The high costs of post-secondary education, the difficulties of young people now emerging into adulthood in finding steady or long-term employment, and the frequency of marriage breakdown are forcing families back into intergenerational models in which adult children often live at home much longer than they used to, or return, singled, with children. At the same time, the rising cost of elder-care and the insufficiency of community resources to supply services is returning the care of the old to families too. This, along with the widespread incidence of fatal and epidemic diseases such as AIDS, may mean that families will be involved in nursing care. Futurists suggest that family homes will need to have "dying rooms" as well as living rooms, and "bounce back" rooms for family members recovering from marriage failure or job loss.

None of these changes is particularly comfortable. But Christians, of all people, should have the resources to respond to—at the very least—the needs within their own families. The call to modest living is being heard by many, in many ways. How to respond to that call, how to readjust values and reeducate tastes, and how to learn new habits and acquire new attitudes: that is the subject of the chapters that follow.

Chapter Two

The Golden Mean

Television brings us the pictures, but somehow it takes a personal encounter before I can understand the concept of the kind of deep poverty that two-thirds of the world lives in. I capture it better when it is put in word-pictures than I do from the television clips: Marilyn, returning after a couple of years in Haiti, saying, "You simply can't imagine how people, average people, live there. The average person expects to get maybe three meals *a week."*

"A week?" I echo, hoping she has made a mistake.

"A week," she reiterates. And I realize that, although I have known times when buying the weekly groceries was a challenge in faith and careful management, our family has always had three meals a day.

Or Cam's descriptions of the two- or three-room farm homes he stayed in during a visit to a farming community in rural Mexico: the sparse tidiness of the best of them, the clutter and grime of the worst, as though there was a fear of throwing anything away in case it might, someday, be needed; the general despair of life ever being more than a struggle for daily subsistence. And I realize that, although I have lived in small farm homes, most of the Mexicans with whom Cam visited would have found them more than adequate, even spacious.

Or Wanjiku Kironyo's descriptions of the women's groups she works with in the Mathare Valley, the huge slum city that is the shadow-city to Nairobi in Kenya: women for whom the main concern is to find some other way to support their children than by brewing potently addictive cheap beer or prostitution; women for whom the important issues are whether they can feed their children, let alone supply shoes and school fees to keep their children in school. And I realize that, although I know what it is to wonder how I am going to afford winter overshoes for growing feet, I have never really wondered *if* they would have footwear or fees for school.

And so, in discussing "modest living," we run into an immediate difficulty. Just what is it? "Modest" compared with what? Where do we draw the line? At what point do we say "satisfied"? And by whose standard of comparison are we entitled to call our lifestyle modest? Do we measure our lifestyle against that of the Haitians? Or the hungry of North Africa or Bangladesh? Yet, how can we ignore the economic realities of the Western world which have given us such a high standard of living? Do we have to live in either self-inflicted poverty or self-induced guilt?

Stanley Tam, a highly successful businessman who has lived modestly and devoted his business profits to Christian causes, makes this telling comment:

> I am not a sackcloth-and-ashes Christian. We have a modest but comfortable home. My wife and I dress well. We are careful with money, never lavish in our spending. . . . It is characteristic of Americans — too often including American Christians — to adjust their living standards to their amount of income, usually keeping the former just a bit higher than the latter. But really, in this land which offers so much, where the poorest family in almost any community has more than the wealthiest family in some overseas areas . . . the thinking Christian needs to consider carefully that point at which he will be willing to say, "It is good enough."[1]

How do we, individually and as families, avoid becoming sackcloth-and-ashes Christians and yet enter into the joys of modest living? The voice of Wisdom speaks to us from the Book of Proverbs: "Give me neither poverty nor riches; but give me only my daily bread." The dangers of either extreme are summarized in the same proverb: "Otherwise, I may have too much and disown You and say, 'Who is the Lord?' Or I may become poor and steal, and so dishonor the name of God" (Prov. 30:8-9).

In wealth, the danger is independence of God. In poverty, the danger is a discouragement so profound that we are tempted to "curse God and die" as Job's wife suggested doing (Job 2:9).

What we are looking for in this whole consideration of modest living is something like the ancient Greek philosophical idea of the golden mean, that perfect balance point at which there is neither too much nor too little of anything. The New Testament refines this concept, telling us that, as believers, a hallmark should be "moderation" (Phil. 4:5). As believers, we have not only the challenge, but the indwelling power of the Holy Spirit, to enable us to live at that golden mean so long sought by the philosophers, that golden mean at which we have neither too much nor too little, but at which we have brought needs and supply into a comfortable balance. In our affluent society, that golden mean or balance point will probably best be reached through generous sharing of the good things with which we have been blessed.

Before we begin feeling a bit smug about the level at which we establish our own personal golden mean, we need to remind ourselves of the golden standard by which all giving, all cutting back, all sharing, must ultimately be measured:

For you know the grace of our Lord Jesus Christ, that though He was rich, yet for your sakes He became poor, so that you through His poverty might become rich (2 Cor. 8:9).

Establishing a Standard of Living

I suggest three basic principles which might serve as a guide as we try to establish at what point in our standard of living we can reasonably say, "It is enough."

1. *Responsibility:* The concept of stewardship of all of our personal resources is central to any meaningful Christian commitment. And, of course, the idea that all we have is a gift to be held in trust carries with it the concept of accountability for the responsible use of those gifts. Paul writes what would have been known as common knowledge in a society where stewards managed large estates: "Now it is required that those who have been given a trust must prove faithful" (1 Cor. 4:2). To be a Christian is to operate in every area of life as a bonded person: one to whom money — or talents, or abilities, or opportunities — can be safely given in trust.

The Scriptures are full of the idea that the way in which we deal with material goods is, fundamentally, a spiritual matter. As I prepared to write this book, I read through the entire New Testament, marking every passage dealing with money or our attitude toward things with a yellow highlighter. I take up that old Bible now, and am still amazed to see how many pages are marked. The writers of Scripture have a great deal to say about material things. According to Harold J. Sutton, "Money and possessions are allotted much space in the Bible. In the Old Testament, it is one verse in six; in the New Testament it is one verse in seven. Sixteen of the parables of our Lord have to do with the stewardship of possessions."[2]

The parable that Jesus told about a lord's entrustment of his servants with varying amounts of money, weighed out in "talents," as told in Matthew's Gospel in chapter 25:14-30, is Jesus' classic discourse on the requirements and responsibilities of stewardship. What we are given we are responsible to use — not solely or even primarily for our own satisfaction — but for maximum profit to the Giver. The implication for those of us living in the wealthy northern half of the world is that we will have to answer for our use of that wealth. There are questions we have to confront — now or at some later judgment time: To what degree have we squandered it? Dug a hole and hid it, failing to invest it in improving the lives of others? Or have we recognized the trust which is ours and used whatever resources have been placed at our disposal wisely, investing not only for material, but also for spiritual returns?

The story Jesus told about entrustment may also be read to remind us that it is the right of the Master to give varying amounts in trust to his servants. From the letters of Paul and James, it is evident that rich and poor people met together in the early churches. (You might like to look at, for example, 1 Corinthians 11:18-22 and James 2:1-4 — passages which discuss courtesy and social sensitivity in an economically mixed situation, and 2 Corinthians 8:1-15 and James 2:14-17 for some discussion of what the apostles taught as the appropriate Christian response to the needs of others within the community.) Individual responsibility for meeting one's own needs and the needs of one's family is stressed in balance with an open-hearted and open-handed response to the needy beyond the immediate circle of family or even of only the local church. It will be in this context of individual and group responsibility that we will one day give account for the management of the material resources entrusted to us, as Jesus' teaching on the judgment of the nations as "sheep" or "goats" clearly shows (Matt. 25:31-46).

Modest living means that there is no financial state in which the responsibility of giving is lifted from us. The reality of this is borne out in a story recorded in Mark's Gospel. Jesus stood watching as people brought their money gifts to the temple. After a number of wealthy people had made large, clinking donations, a poverty-stricken widow put in two "very small copper coins." And Jesus said, "I tell you the truth, this poor widow has put more into the treasury than all the others. They all gave out of their wealth; but she, out of her poverty, put in everything — all she had to live on" (Mark 12:43-44). Jesus enunciated a principle of reality in the kingdom of God: that our giving is not measured by the amount we give, but by the amount we have left over when we have given. Giving from our wealth and plenty is one kind of giving, but giving from our poverty, sharing our "daily bread," is the kind of giving especially commended by the One whom, as Christians, we call Lord. Realism demands that we learn the deep pain and great joy of establishing a standard of giving that affects our standard of living.

2. *Restraint:* Living modestly by choice means making decisions about spending and giving that establish our standard of living somewhere below the level we could enjoy if our income were administered entirely for the needs and desires of ourselves and of our families.

People who choose to live modestly refuse to be coerced by television and other advertising into feeling that everything five years or older is obsolete and in need of replacement. When shopping to replace our fifteen-year-old living room furniture (which, in the end, we decided to reupholster rather than replace), we were startled to be told that the average North American family refurnishes major areas of a home every four to five years. Actually, I expect that's more wishful thinking on the part of furniture-makers than an actual reality . . . or maybe we're living even farther behind — or below — the average than I have realized.

A visit to countries in which living and business is carried on in buildings many hundred years old is a sobering corrective for our North American "new is better" mentality, where the swinging demolition ball is a symbol of progress. Friends of ours who have spent their lives in Europe have pointed out to us that our feeling that a car is "old" simply on the basis of its year or mileage is also idiosyncratically North American, out of line with the thinking in much of the rest of the world. "There's nothing wrong with the upholstery, is there?" our friend asked, walking around our ancient half-ton truck. "And the exterior is not rusted out, is it? So what if it has 150,000 miles on it? There's nothing that can't be fixed to make it run another 100,000 miles. A car like this wouldn't be considered old in Europe." Let alone in Mexico, we have come to realize, or in the Caribbean or South America.

Living with restraint means planning rather than impulse

buying; assessing "wish lists" to discriminate between needs and wants; and evaluating one's own needs and desires in the light of the needs of others. That's no easy matter, since probably every purchase we make could be scrutinized by someone and found to be excessive. It means living in some kind of uneasy tension between the *via positiva* — the way of grateful celebration of the good things of life, and the *via negativa* — the way of self-abnegation and self-emptying on behalf of others. In learning to live under the principle of restraint in our spending habits, we have to resist not only the voices that tell us, "Want it? Buy it," but also the voices that tell us that everything delightful borders on the sinful, that we should not enjoy the good things of life. It is precisely in the matter of sharing our material goods that the Apostle John writes, "If our hearts do not condemn us, we have confidence before God" (1 John 3:21). Living with restraint means that, having worked out a decision to buy in the light of the principles of responsibility and restraint, we need not live in continual guilt about the things we do decide to buy, but in joyful, grateful enjoyment.

And living with restraint may mean that we are free to make at least some of our decisions on some basis other than economic maximization. A job that may have high earning potential may be turned down for one in which one earns less but is doing work that is more satisfying, more fully fulfilling one's deep sense of vocation or call. Some of these considerations were involved when, after we had reestablished our personal finances and repaid our debts, Cam and I spent a lot of time pondering how we should order the second half of our adult lives. The road of economic maximization was clear: We could both get teaching jobs, hold them for another twenty years, and rent out the farmland as an additional source of income. But Cam's love for the land and his deep vocation or call to nurture life — not to mention his penchant for risk-taking — called him into a new commitment to his farming as a full-time occupation. My hunger for learning and my need to write, as well as to do some part-time teaching, called me to go back to the university for graduate work. And so we again combined precarious income sources, needing to continually exercise tight-reined fiscal management and restraint. But we wake up every morning with the exhilaration of knowing that we are both able to do what we love to do, what we are called to do. And, we remind ourselves, our seven-year-old car is still not old by world standards.

The restraint in spending that we learned in very hard times has become a matter of choice, with the result that we have had more freedom in making career choices than many of our age-mates. Recently, when considering and turning down a "steady job," I found myself saying, "Since I'm willing to be poor, I am free to go on exploring." Being free to choose to continue contract and freelance work with all of its uncertainty and challenge was an outcome of having learned to live within the constraints of uncertain income. And even though we sometimes chafe at the restrictions of living within a limited and unpredictable income, Cam and I realize that we are quite wonderfully free.

3. *Realism:* Living modestly requires a strong sense of realism, something which is often dulled by easy credit and high-pressure advertising. It means living within our budgets, whether they are limited by necessity or by choice. With accessible credit and continual inducements to buy, it is possible for a family to live beyond its means, keeping up an appearance of prosperity in excess of real earnings, at least for a period of time.

Modest living also means living with a sense of realism and responsibility toward those to whom we owe money. We are under the same instructions as were given to the Christians in ancient Thessalonica — to live "so that your daily life may win the respect of outsiders," — meaning to conduct our business in a way which is aboveboard in the eyes of the larger community (1 Thes. 4:12). The name of our Lord has been made light of and the effectiveness of the church has been seriously impaired by the cavalier attitude of many who call themselves Christians in matters of business ethics. "My dad always warned me to look out for anyone carrying a Bible," a neighbor told me, and I felt sad as I acknowledged that many nonbelieving people have higher standards when it comes to conducting their business affairs than do some who call themselves by the name, "Christian." *Realism* in our business affairs means, at the very least, honoring incurred debts and operating ethically and honestly in all of our business affairs.

Realism also means recognizing the needs of those who depend upon us. "If anyone does not provide for his relatives, and especially his immediate family, he has denied the faith and is worse than an unbeliever" is Paul's strong statement on the matter (1 Tim. 5:8). We must realistically provide for the needs of our children and of aged members of our families. Such provision has an indisputable *a priori* claim on our finances. Some of Jesus' harshest words were said to those who excused themselves from obligations to their aging parents by claiming that their money was "Corban," or dedicated to a religious purpose (as described in Mark 7:11-12). As we more and more frequently encounter the neglect of old people by their families, we need to live out our faith in honoring the needs of our own kin. There is truth in the old folk saying that "Charity begins at home." Realistically, if charity—not in the sense of pity or duty, but in the practice of need-meeting love—does not start there, it does not start at all.

Basically, then, modest living is an orientation toward income and standard of living rather than any specific point on the line between poverty and wealth. No single inflexible standard can be set, for what is modest living for people with large earning power may still be out of reach for others with less. The concept of modest living does not suggest that there is anything wrong with enjoying the good things of life as they are entrusted to us. I have composed psalms of thanksgiving—admittedly, some of them quite mawkish, but nonetheless sincere—for my automatic household appliances, grateful for the hours they have freed up from household chores for other pursuits. I still rejoice as I lift clothes out of the perma-press cycle of a clothes drier, realizing that I have written books in the hours that previous generations of women spent at the scrub board and the ironing board.

While we lived in a very cramped rented house, Cam and I looked forward to God's provision of a home big enough for our family of four fast-growing children. He did supply that home. We planned it with loving, prayerful care, making careful modifications to make a modest standard plan meet the particular needs of our family. And when the house was built, we moved into it (with, I remember so well, our two preschoolers with chicken pox and no hot water turned on yet) with thanksgiving and joy that have never stopped. It was perhaps just because we waited so long to have a home of our own, or perhaps because we built modestly enough to be able to feel not a single pang of guilt and to be able to pay off the mortgage in ten years, or perhaps because the plan we chose and modified has suited our family needs so well that we have to feel the Lord heard our request for divine guidance while we labored over the plans. Or perhaps just because for us it is, finally, home. Whatever the mix, our little white-stuccoed bungalow with chocolate brown trim has been a source of great joy and much praise.

In the process of buying our home, as in our other expenditures over the years, we have learned that nagging feelings of guilt about physical comforts disappear if the good things we have are not had at the expense of others; and if the good things we enjoy are truly within our means and are not just a result of setting ourselves adrift on a sea of credit.

Modest living is not so much a renunciation of specific things in themselves as it is a refusal to make things a goal in life or a source of ultimate satisfaction. It is the exercise of *responsibility, restraint,* and *realism:* whether our means are large or small.

Neither Poverty nor Riches

People who have lived cross-culturally have found that the general level of unhappiness seems to be nearly as great in affluent North America as in poverty-stricken countries of the world. Perhaps it is just a reality that too much money makes people as miserable as too little, that there is perhaps a happy medium at which basic needs can be met without undue anxiety, but at which that endless list of things-to-be-had is simply out of reach. Such a happy medium might be something close to the "golden mean," that balance point most conducive to human happiness.

It is a struggle to find such a balance point in our economic lives. Perhaps we will only begin our search for it when we realize that the only real satisfactions in life can never come from things — no matter how many or how lovely. Real satisfaction comes from relationships, of which the central and most deeply satisfying one is to be in communion with our Creator.

We are invited into such a relationship — the one for which we most deeply yearn and yet for which we so often attempt to substitute the procurement of things — through a life-changing, life-shaping commitment to Jesus.

Where might we start in re-evaluating our attitudes toward things? The Bible word — the word that Jesus proclaimed — is "Repent, for the kingdom of heaven is near" (Matt. 4:17). *Repent* does not mean to weep, or to "come forward" in a meeting — although it may be manifested in such actions or emotions. *Repent* means, simply, to make an about-face, a 180-degree change of direction. It means to turn away from what we have been seeking and to look in an entirely different direction for our sense of meaning and satisfaction in life. We might pray something like this:

> *Creator God, You made this good world and everything in it. I admit to You that I have too often been caught up in the things You have made and too little concerned with knowing, loving, and serving You. Forgive me, I pray. I want to know You more fully and love You more wholly — and to be set free from my preoccupation with things — no matter how legitimate they may seem to be in themselves. Through Jesus Christ Your Son and my Lord, I pray.*

Chapter Three

Contentment: Learned, Not Earned

I was pulling up to a stop sign recently when I heard the commentator on the radio discussing a poll in which people had been asked how much money they felt they needed to earn in order to be comfortable. I did a quick mental calculation and had a figure in mind when the voice on the radio went on to say, "Most people felt they needed exactly double what they are now earning in order to be content."

I had to laugh at myself: the figure I had calculated in my mind was just that—double what last year's income tax figure had been. I fit right into the stereotype the survey had discovered, sharing the prevalent discontent—or, at the very least, disequilibrium—with the status quo. As my sister-in-law Marg pointed out to me many years ago, even the Apostle Paul had to say, "I have *learned* to be content" (Phil. 4:11, emphasis added). "Maybe it didn't come any easier to Paul to be content than it does to me," Marg said, "but it is a lesson that can be learned."

Contentment Can Be Learned
Contentment does not come easily to our hearts. I suppose from the very moment that the human heart lost communion with the Creator, we have all tried to stuff that empty yearning with things: things desired, things worked for, things even

worshiped. So contentment does not just come naturally to most of us. But it can be learned.

Contentment is probably the closest state we can reach to something like happiness. It is a quiet plateau that can be reached internally even when there seems little external reason for it. I remember visiting with Brian and Laura, a farm family, on a neighboring farm before Cam and I were married. The kitchen was sparse in a way I didn't know still existed — like something out of *Little House on the Prairie,* but this was 1960, not 1890. The kitchen was dominated by the wood stove, on which the cooking was still done; most of the chairs pulled out to the plain wood table had no backs. But the farm wife cheerfully served hot, black coffee and fresh buns, and the husband talked about life with a serenity I have only rarely encountered. Clearly, Brian and Laura had learned contentment.

But I have found it to be a difficult lesson to learn, and one which I have to relearn from time to time. In our affluent society, we live with the continual delusion that with "just one thing more" (or double our current income), we would be perfectly content. And so we are kept perpetually unhappy, perpetually off-balance, perpetually more concerned about things than we are about the more important issues of life — like our relationships with each other and with God.

"If only we had—" is an ongoing game of fill-in-the-blank. We discover through life that as we move into that bigger house, earn that larger income, wear those more stylish clothes, we are still the same discontent people — still being urged, as were our first parents in the Garden, to desire, and reach, and take.

When I first wrote this book, my own children were small, and I told this story:

> As I am writing these lines, my four-year-old is speaking to me from the kitchen where he is folding up newspapers he had spread out on the floor for spatter painting. "What is it, Mitchell?" I call.

He walks into the room where I am typing, holding a folded newspaper and studying an ad wistfully. "I wish we had a snowmobile," he says. And I sigh deep down inside, realizing how hard it is for those of our rich generation to enter the kingdom of spiritual values and to really understand how little *things* do mean.

My memory flashes back to the days, soon after we had completed our studies at the university, when Cam thought aloud, "I wish I had a snowmobile." They were fairly new on the popular market then, and in our long, snowy winters it's not hard to rationalize a "need" for such a recreational vehicle. Cam was earning a good wage; he was entitled to what our nephew Terry once called "a man's toy." But it wasn't long before the possibilities of the "toy" were exhausted. And every snowdrift started to look like every other snowdrift, and every race to feel like every other race. The snowmobile—finally sold to someone else—stands in our minds as a lifelong reminder of how unsatisfying individual things are.

Now it is our granddaughters who look yearningly at the catalogs and say, "I wish I had . . . ," and the sigh I sigh is the same. How hard, how very hard it is for us or for our little ones to find contentment in an affluent, thing-clogged world.

Nor is the problem anything new. David Grayson, the pseudonymous author of *Adventures in Contentment,* a quaint and interesting book published in 1906 and given to me by an elderly "gentleman farmer" of our district, tells how, from the age of seventeen, Grayson was driven "always forward, toward that vague Success which we Americans love to glorify." Then a serious illness arrested him, and he moved into a much slower existence. He says,

> I remember walking in the sunshine, weak yet, but curiously satisfied. I that was dead lived again. . . . And I possessed . . . a knowledge of a former exis-

tence, which I knew, even then, I could never return to.[1]

His basic discoveries on which he built this contentment were:

> That we are not, after all, the slaves of things . . .
> that we are not the used, but the users; that life is
> more than profit or loss.[2]

Contentment, as expressed by this young man, and by others whom I know who have had close scrapes with death, is really a matter of living "on the other side of death." For the early Christians, the experience of baptism was a physical enactment of their entering into Christ's death, burial, and resurrection (see Rom. 6:3-4). As the new believers came up from the baptismal waters, hair and face streaming, they were dramatizing their entry into a new life, a life lived on the other side of death. Surely this is the image — as well as the reality — which lies behind Paul's words to the Colossian believers:

> Since, then, you have been raised with Christ, set your
> hearts on things above, where Christ is seated at the
> right hand of God. Set your minds on things above, not
> on earthly things. For you died, and your life is now
> hidden with Christ in God (Col. 3:1-3).

Each summer, when our small village church gathers as a family for a weekend of fellowship at a sapphire-blue northern lake, its shape carved by glacial ice and its waters cold all summer, we celebrate the coming-to-faith of new believers with that ancient rite of baptism. The dramatic reenactment of God's act of grace in uniting each of us with our Lord in His death, and through Him bringing us into new life, reestablishes perspective and sharpens the focus for all of us. As the soaked and chilled confessors stumble back to the shore, we wade out to meet them, to wrap them in towels and in our arms. Risen to new life, made part of a new family, welcomed to the sandy shore—as one day we will be welcomed by those who have gone before us, when we go through that final baptism of death and find ourselves risen, washed and new in that final realization of "home" and "family" that is heaven. We who welcome the new believers into the community of faith are reminded again of our own baptismal confessions, of the newness of life into which we have entered—and are, each time, challenged anew to consider that since we have died, and our life has been "hidden with Christ in God," we have an invitation—and an obligation—to live with our hearts and minds set on "things above" rather than on the things and toys of this life.

Some of us—like me—are slow learners. We seem to have to "die" a little every day. Perhaps there are ways of shortening the learning process, of leaping to the mature understanding of how trivial things of this world are and how meaningless are the little toys for which we strive and struggle. For David Grayson, mentioned earlier, the shortcut was a face-off with death itself. For some it may be a dark night of the soul in which we learn full surrender and cry out, "All that I have and am and want, I give to You, my Lord and Master." Perhaps for the rest of us it has to be a matter of taking the things one at a time, as they present themselves to our minds in a delusion of delight, and dying to them—literally dying to the desire for that particular thing. And then, as one thing after another is passed by and we die to the desire that was kindled within us, we will gradually reach a habit of laying things before God without the long struggle of soul.

Cam and I call this attitude "holding things on an open hand."

We remember how one of our children had, as a toddler, clutched a piece of candy we had told her not to take. Such defiant, tightly curled little round fingers! We think of how we had to pry those little fingers, one by one, away from that treasure. It would have been so much easier for her—and for us—if she had held it out to us on an open hand and let us take it.

Job showed the attitude of "holding things on an open hand"

when he cried out, "The Lord gave, and the Lord has taken away; may the name of the Lord be praised" (Job 1:21). The earlier in life we learn to stop grabbing, clutching, and holding tightly, and the sooner we learn to hold all of life's good things in an open hand, the more easily and gently God can deal with us as His children. That's another way of saying that the more we live "on the other side of death," as Paul describes it in Romans 6, the less we will be attached to temporal, material things.

I will always remember the Sunday when the usher on our aisle in church held the offering basket out to our family. He noticed that little Heather Ruth, barely two at the time, was clutching something tightly. Assuming that she had been given money to be put in the plate, he held the basket quietly in front of her. Blue-eyed, round-cheeked Heather looked gravely from the plate to the usher, then down to her tightly clenched fist. And then, just as gravely, she moved her hand over the offering plate and let go what she was holding. The usher was as startled as I was to see, lying in the offering basket, a tiny paper figure of a blue-swaddled baby Moses—a treasured item from the take-home things she had been given in Sunday School. We smiled—but with tears just back of our eyes—for Heather had opened her hand to give something very precious to her.

I have found in many instances that God has waited patiently for us to move some desire from a position of central importance to the fringes of our minds—in short, no matter how reasonable or precious, to let it go—before letting us have that very item. He seems to grant "things" only when we are living relative to them, "on the other side of death," dead to them as goals, as status symbols, as sources of satisfaction, and accepting them only as means of bringing pleasure and praise to the One who has created all things (see Rev. 4:11).

Maybe one of the deepest instincts in a woman is a nesting instinct: a desire to have a suitable place in which to raise her brood. As a European friend put it: "For myself, I care not at all about things. Pff! You can have anything I have; I do not care. But for my children, it is different. Children make one bourgeois." This instinct is right and proper. Yet, like all of our good basic instincts, it can be turned against us and against God if we do not guard our lives carefully. Our need for a nesting place can become an obsession. Our definition of "adequate" can be raised to levels to which we may really have no right—merely by turning the pages of *Better Homes and Gardens* or by driving through those mouth-watering "exclusive" areas of our cities.

When we moved out to the old farmhouse where Cam had been raised, I said to him, "Don't ever ask me to move again." I put my roots down, right alongside the towering pine that stood close to the front veranda. The house was old, at least in western Canadian terms. It had been built soon after the turn of the century, and a lean-to had been added somewhere along the way. The kitchen occupied the lean-to, with a floor so sloped that anything which spilled landed up against the south baseboards. Upstairs were two bedrooms, both built under the eaves with steeply sloping walls; a tiny niche which in the old days had been—in the most strictly limited sense of the word—a *bathroom*, just big enough for an old-fashioned tub, and a walk-in closet or "drying room" with a tiny windowed dormer. Into this upstairs we tucked ourselves with first three and then four children, turning the niche into crib space and later building a double-decker bunk into it and painting and papering the "drying room" to make a tiny bedroom off ours.

There were saving virtues about the old place with its torn screens and loose windowpanes. Such as a large living room which, despite a sagging ceiling that made us wonder just what day the upstairs would come downstairs, had a fieldstone fireplace; a lovely big bathroom-utility room on the main floor, created out of one of the downstairs bedrooms when the house had been "modernized" late in its career. And, best of all, a downstairs bedroom adjoining the living room that worked perfectly for a study-office for me. Outside, the old house was peeling, the veranda sagging. But inside, there was warmth and love and happiness. And while I racked my brains trying to think of ways to expand our living space around the needs of our growing children, I had no intention of moving. Ever.

And then Cam, who had been increasingly distressed with a continuous hay fever reaction, went to an allergist. Skin tests were done, and the allergist was ready with his diagnosis. "Do you by any chance live in an old house?" he asked. Cam nodded. Yes, we lived in an old house.

"Ah!" the allergist exclaimed. "There's your problem. You are allergic to the sort of molds which accumulate between the walls of old houses, especially walls where moisture can seep in. Your strongest reaction is to such molds. I strongly advise that you get into a new house."

(I was shocked, some years after the publication of the first edition of this book, to discover that an editor who had worked on the manuscript had envisioned these molds as something visible growing *on* our walls — like some kind of fungus or moss. Please understand: these were invisible molds, growing *between* the walls — not on the outside of them. Had they been visible, we would have tried to solve our problem with a scrub brush and a good strong disinfectant!)

The doctor's diagnosis and prescription shattered my contentment. If Cam was sick in the house we lived in, and if a new house was necessary to his good health, wasn't it obvious that the Lord had indicated that we should build a new house? Obvious — to me. Not so obvious, unfortunately, to Cam.

Because what was more obvious to Cam than it was to me was that the business was going badly. That we were selling cattle at a loss. That we had debts that were going to be hard to meet. And Cam could not face building a new house — even on doctor's orders — while telling people that he could not afford to pay his bills. And so we were stalemated. For perhaps the first time in our marriage, our ability to communicate and to come to an understanding seemed to break down completely.

And then, the Lord provided us with a house.

Not, like in some people's stories, a big, new house that somehow a kindly rich person had a sudden need to sell at some inexplicably low price, although, believe me, I imagined such provision as I prayed. Nothing like that. God provided an *old* house, squarer and better built than our previous one, even more picturesque, and for rent. I, who had framed my request to the Lord as my "Three S Prayer" — for space, settledness, and security — found myself moving from one old farmhouse to another old farmhouse about a third smaller; from one where I felt sure I could live out my life, to one in which we would have three months' notice if a member of the landlord's family needed it; from one which we owned, to one which we could only rent. Talk about insecurity! I felt like a hen that couldn't quite settle back on the nest for fear it might suddenly be jerked away from under her.

If the tears had flowed as I walked down the winter lane of our own home, trying to figure out how to cope with Cam's illness and adamantine attitude about building a new home, now I found tears starting without notice as I tried to get things tucked into this latest domicile. I somehow could not reconcile myself to this as God's way of answering my prayer.

To make things worse, the house we moved into had a "reputation." It had belonged to a well-to-do city businessman who lived in the country. And since it was set well back from the road, down a pine-lined drive and in a beautiful parklike yard, people thought I was wonderfully lucky to be moving into such a grand house. "That's a beautiful big old house," they would comment.

"Beautiful, yes," I would reply. But big, definitely not. My hardest adjustment was having no study to work in. My filing cabinets were out in the unheated veranda; my desk and typewriter were stuffed into our small bedroom alongside the bed. That was harder for me to cope with than the ten-by-thirteen-foot combination kitchen-dining room with *five* doors leading off it. Or the bats that did not always stay up in the attic.

Why? Why? Why? What could possibly make this move right? Trying to make the best of things, I buoyed myself up through each week. We had moved closer to the center of the farming operation, so Cam could be home for lunch and supper with us. That was good, especially since for the previous two years he had left early in the morning and not returned until 10 P.M. or later at night all through the cropping season, becoming a virtual stranger to the children. And his allergy symptoms were definitely less acute. I was grateful for those things. Yet, each Sunday, when the kids had excused themselves after dinner and were out playing in the yard and Cam and I still sat across the table that took up about half of the tiny—although very pretty and freshly painted—kitchen, the tears would come. And the questions. And the anger. Cam was unmovable. He could not see how we could afford to build a house at that time.

And then one Sunday afternoon, I walked away from the table in anger. There wasn't very far that I could go in the house to get away from Cam, but I went into the bedroom adjoining the kitchen and threw myself, sobbing, onto the bed. And then, as I quieted, things began to come into focus for me.

Such unhappiness, I knew, was not coming from the Lord. I was angry and rebellious and wretchedly unhappy. And then, the gift of imagination helped me see into a possible future. I imagined what it would be like if I did coerce Cam into complying with my wish for a new home. Suppose we went ahead and built? Suppose then, that as Cam now feared, the house became a fearful financial burden? Suddenly I could picture us growing apart in a house big enough for us to really get apart from each other, with our love killed by my demands. And just imagining any size or shape of house without the love and joy which, through all the "better or worse" situations since we had been married, had been our mainstay, was convincing to me.

I prayed, then, something like this: *I don't feel like accepting this situation, Lord. It seems upside-down to me. It seems to me that we need a home now—not someday when the kids are grown and gone. But I am willing to wait for You to communicate that need to Cam without my demanding or badgering.* I felt like I was dying, and on that particular issue, I was.

When at last my weeping was over and my heart felt calm,

yet still very sore from the struggle, I went back to the kitchen.

Cam was still sitting there, nursing a cup of now-cold tea with a hurt and bewildered, angry look on his face. I sat down across from him and reached for his hand—a big, square, capable hand I had loved at first sight so many years before. "Cam," I said, "I'm all finished. I've said everything I'm going to say about 'house.' You won't hear me say that word again until you say it first."

And then I found myself "living on the other side of death" on that particular matter. Joy began to flow back into my life.

The little house was no less crowded, but now I could enjoy its charm and beauty. No longer threatened by my demands, Cam was able to begin to share his problems and concerns with me, and communication between us gradually became the deep, intimate sharing we had known before. I learned, again, that love and contentment are all that are really necessary to turn an "inadequate" house into a happy home.

The next few months fully vindicated Cam's determination not to assume any further debt for a house. When the farming business failed—an outcome that I had not realized was as imminent as Cam had—we were set to weather a financial storm that could have capsized us had we also been trying to pay for a new home. Our personal credibility with our creditors was high because we were living stringently, and they were remarkably patient with us. The little rented house was inexpensive, which helped to keep our living costs to a minimum. And all through that winter, the long hard winter of psychological restoration after a business failure, we thanked God for our snug and inexpensive accommodation. Debt we faced. Problems we had. But, as we lived close together in the small house, we experienced the joy of simple things: of enough money to buy a week's groceries, of enough money to pay the month's rent, of peace and joy and love between ourselves. What might have been "the winter of our discontent"—apart from the transforming work of the Holy Spirit—we shall always remember as the winter of recovery and healing.

In our financial setback, the Lord weeded out from Cam's heart, one by one, things that may have become too dear to him. The big tractors and trucks and equipment had to be sold as we liquidated assets to try to cover liabilities. And, at the same time, just as relentlessly, the great Gardener weeded from my heart the need, the burning desire, for a big new house.

We are still in the process of learning "how to get along happily whether [we] have much or little." But on some matters, at least, we are living on the other side of death. I do not want to give the impression that the learning process has been fun, or the lessons learned easily. But the Spirit of God is a thorough and loving Teacher. And, since all the other joys of life are actually dependent upon contentment, it is contentment we need most to learn.

At any level of income we can be inwardly gnawed by discontent. Most of us are still tricked into thinking we would be comfortable at just double our current rate of earning. But probably you have encountered, as I have, those few people who—apparently regardless of level of income—enjoy quiet contentment. From these encounters, I have become convinced that contentment cannot be earned. But I also know—from painful experience that has opened out onto lasting joy—that, even by such a slow learner as I, contentment can be learned.

Chapter Four

Living on Love

You cannot live on love. But it is even harder to live without it. And when a family—by choice or necessity—cuts back its standard of living, it needs to work at raising its standard of loving. Economic hardship is an experience that serves to prove, and to improve, love more than any other experience can. Of course, it often works the other way too. Economic problems are cited as a major contributing factor to a great many marriage breakdowns.[1]

So, if you are facing financial restructuring—for whatever reasons—you need to make sure your marriage is weather-proofed for the storms. Clear and honest communication becomes extremely important at such times. When people feel called to exercise restraint in their spending in order to give more, or to improve their quality of life by having time for other priorities—or just to get out of debt and start over—they need to work out the details of their situation carefully and come to an agreement about how they are going to cut their spending. If a husband and wife do not fully share the goals for which they are reducing their standard of living, and come to agreement about the extent of that reduction, it is hard to avoid bitterness. When Bob, a prosperous dentist, decided to give up his practice to assume a church-related ministry, his wife found the "call" hard to accept.

"Is it a full-time job he's going to?" I asked.

"Yes," she told me. "At a half-time salary." She went along with the change, but with little joy in the new status quo.

No matter how altruistic we may be in our ideals, we have to go on making our way in some sector of the culture in which we live. Crushing financial worries are no blessing. Nor is continual tension or arguing about what constitutes a legitimate expenditure. And because money-making and money-disposing are so tightly tied up with self-esteem in our culture, money discussions may need to be prefaced with an assurance: "We're not talking about each other, and we're not talking about our marriage. We're talking about how we are going to organize our finances." Cam calls this "putting the issue out on the table" — separating the discussion from ourselves and, as much as possible, from potentially explosive emotional elements. Most of us have learned (by communications training or by hard experience) that it is wiser to send "I" messages: "I feel as though you disapprove of the way I am handling the grocery budget," rather than "you" messages: "You always act as though I spend too much for groceries." Careful listening to each other, with feedback loops like, "Do I hear you saying . . . " and, sometimes, the decision to postpone a discussion until both parties are more rested or under less immediate pressure can help to moderate the "climate" of painful but necessary discussions.

If the cutback is not one of choice, but one which is forced upon you, then clear and complete honesty in communications becomes even more imperative. As long as either partner tries to pretend that there are no problems, that life can go on as it has been, the family will live in a position which is at odds with reality and which is therefore untenable. Honesty with each other is a necessary prerequisite to honesty with the outside world.

Family Communication
When there are children in the family, some of the communication has to be with them. They should not be loaded with worrisome details, but they need to understand the general

outline of the reality the family is facing.

As the condition of our business gradually became public knowledge — and there are few secrets that can be kept in a rural community — our children had to field questions from friends at school. One day, Geoffrey, then nine, came into the house.

"Dad," he asked, sounding extra casual, "is our company going broke?"

"Why?" Cam asked.

"Well, because Grant told me it was folding up."

"He's right, Geoff," Cam replied.

"What does that mean?"

Cam explained carefully but simply to Geoff the way in which cattle-market conditions and a killing August frost on our crops had worked together to bring the company to a position where it was unable to repay its obligations without selling all of its machinery and other assets.

It isn't easy to say to children, "We just can't afford it," but that year we had to tell our children just that; not only about such things as the Christmas goodies in the stores and catalogs, but about items far more basic, such as winter overshoes.

We simply didn't have the money to outfit all eight feet, and they all needed new boots. So we told the children about the situation, and as a family we prayed about it. Each child prayed for his or her own winter boots, some giving specifications as to the type they would prefer. The Lord answered first by delaying snow. In our Alberta winters, we usually have permanent snow by the first week of November. That winter, no snow fell and stayed until December 22. And by that time, we had received a small check that covered the cost of on-sale overshoes for all eight feet. Not, mind you, the bush boots Geoffrey had requested. Nor the side-zipped tall boots of Cammie's desire.

But, for all the children, warm and acceptably styled winter footwear. The children learned to enjoy the Lord's provision and give thanks along with us. It was an experience for all of us in learning neither to take the good, basic provisions we needed for granted, nor to demand the supply of every whim. And best of all, when we talk together about those days, the children remember them as snug and happy years — not as years of deprivation or hardship.

Dealing with Blame and Anger

Economic pressures do create a need and an opportunity for a family to really pull together. Or a situation in which a family falls apart. When the going gets rough, I expect that everyone has to fight against the desire to lay blame.[2] If only *someone* hadn't made that particular business decision; if only *someone* didn't need to spend so much on clothes. But that "root of bitterness," if ever allowed to develop, will be destructive: if not of the marriage itself, certainly of the love that sustains it. It's like the red-rooted pigweed that we fight in our gardens in the countryside where I live: a tiny plant at first, but one that puts down a long root and sucks the moisture and nutrition away from anything growing near it.

I know I struggled with blaming (sort of like a long game of "pin the tail on the donkey" — any donkey but me). I tried blaming Cam, the neighbor who was our business partner, the markets, the weather. I was too pious, of course, to even think of blaming God. So I was pretty startled one day as I did my daily Scripture reading (for some reason I was plowing my way through the Pentateuch that winter) to be sharply reminded that when Israel complained against Moses, they were actually grumbling against God. This struck me as I read through Exodus. The response of Moses and Aaron to the complaining Israelites was straightforward: "The Lord . . . has heard your grumbling against Him. Who are we, that you should grumble against us?" (Ex. 16:6-7) God's attitude toward His complaining children in the desert is echoed and applied by Paul in the first letter to the Corinthian Christians: "We should not test the Lord, as some of them did. . . . And do not grumble, as some of them did" (1 Cor. 10:9-10).

My complaining was — finally and most honestly — a complaint against God: against Him for having let us get into such a mess. Had we not prayed about each decision we had made? Had we not really desired God's will to be done in our lives and our business? Let's face it, however much we might blame ourselves for some of the decisions we made, our particular circumstances did come directly from God's hand in the form of adverse weather. An ancient psalmist put it like this: "Lightning and hail, snow and clouds, stormy winds . . . do His bidding" (Ps. 148:8) — a pretty sobering thought when you find yourself trying to salvage a ruined crop.

I slowly began to realize that it is more honest and more direct to take our complaints right to God, the way Naomi does at the beginning of the Book of Ruth in the Old Testament. She doesn't say, "Elimelech and I made a terrible mistake." She doesn't say, "The folks back at home, or the government, or somebody out there is responsible." She says: "The Lord has afflicted me; the Almighty has brought misfortune upon me." Like Naomi, Job takes his case right to the highest court, traces the events of his life to the sovereign purposes of God: "The Lord gave and the Lord has taken away" — not, "The Lord gave and the Sabeans have taken away," or "The Lord gave and the firestorm has taken away." No, Job attributes his misfortune, as much as his good fortune, to a sovereign God — and only in that context is he able to say, "May the name of the Lord be praised" (Job 1:21).

Once I quit trying to "protect God" from my anger and frustration and confusion, I could quit blaming Cam and myself and my neighbor and the markets and the weather. I could say, *Lord — I don't get this. I don't know why You would let us be battered like this. But it's happening, so You must have allowed it for purposes I don't begin to understand. Help us to learn what You are trying to teach us. And P.S., Lord, please help us get out of this situation — soon.* I found something out in this struggle: when I quit blaming, Cam quit being defensive, and we began to have more constructive conversations, working together to formulate plans for our financial recovery. One of the really wonderful things about the hard months that long, cold winter after our business failed was that Cam and I actually had "quality time" together. More time to read the Scriptures and pray together than we had had for years. Time for a second cup of tea after supper. Time to pray—sometimes even at some length, in between the interruptions of four small children. The message that came through to us above all the others was very simple and just this: that God is, indeed, our Father. He gives only good gifts to His children—even when the wrapping is unattractive to our eyes.

A memory that sustained me was of my mother after she and my father were involved in a serious car accident. She had been released from the hospital, but her face was still swollen and misshapen, and she had a huge orange and purple bruise over her eyes. Mother could not move without pain, but she sat stiffly on a straight kitchen chair as I prepared a meal. Speaking with difficulty, since it hurt her even to catch a breath, she said in her quiet way, "It doesn't *feel* good, darling, but it must *be* good." It was an articulation of the kind of holding-on faith that my parents lived out before their family. And it's the kind of faith that helped Cam and me to know that behind the threatening clouds of economic reversals shone the sun of God's loving-kindness.

As we tried to sort things out, Cam would say, "The Lord knows, and the Lord knows I don't know." That too was a statement of faith. Just that one fact—that our Heavenly Father *knew,* both our situation and our real needs, material and spiritual—was something to hold onto until we could begin to discern His plans for us, "plans to give . . . hope and a future" (Jer. 29:11) expressed in our difficult circumstances.

Fending off bitterness—or rooting it out wherever we found it—was one kind of emotional and spiritual problem we had to cope with. Depression was another. The summer that we watched our business buckle under day by day, listening to the market reports as cattle prices slipped lower and lower, and then awakening to find our crops destroyed, we both fought depression. I found myself talking with God through sudden and frequent tears. I remember, especially, walking down the tree-lined lane of our rented property. When the poplar leaves were first bursting out of their sticky shells into little twin-kling valentine-shaped leaves, I struggled with having had to move our family into such a tiny house. I felt angry and help-less at our lack of money. I looked up through the new leaves to the sky and prayed, "Lord, none of this makes any sense to me at all. I only know one thing, and that is that *I love You.*" I made this declaration day after day, the spring colors of green and blue often blurred by my tears into a swimming green-blue underwater world where I felt I was drowning.

Then, as summer progressed, and things got worse, I would take the walk down the lane and look up into trees where the full-sized dark-green leaves blotted out the cloud-piled sky. And then I prayed another prayer: "Lord, it's even worse now. I don't know anything at all now." And then the little Sunday School hymn played itself out in my mind: *"Jesus loves me, this I know / For the Bible tells me so."* And I finished my prayer, "I don't know anything at all now, Lord . . . except that *You love me.*" And that is when I quit feeling like I was going to drown. I had found the bottom. Underneath all my grief and confusion there was the rocklike assurance of God's love. Underneath, after all, were the Everlasting Arms. And the love of God became a source, far greater than even our own great love for each other, on which we could draw as we learned to live on love.

Never, in any marriage, is there a time when loving support, deep sharing, and much prayer for a partner are more neces-sary than in such tough times. In easy times, it may be possi-ble to assume each other's love. In hard times, that love needs to be stated and reiterated. Not some kind of phony, artificial love, but love based on the discovery of strengths in each other. The wife can commend the husband's integrity and ap-preciate his concern for his family, while the husband can express appreciation for a wife's frugality and uncomplaining attitude. And love can thrive, for as Samuel Johnson pointed out, it is, after all, "a native of the rocks."

Later, as you pass through the experience together, you may both gain insights that will help you to keep the trauma from repeating itself. Under the guidance of the Holy Spirit and with all of His dovelike tenderness, a wife and a husband may minister to each other as they see weaknesses develop under the strain, or as they come to understand personal weakness that produced the strain in the first place. It becomes a matter of spiritual and personal survival to keep on "building up yourselves in your most holy faith" (Jude 20).

Preparing to Learn

As you commend each other's strengths and tenderly minister to each other's weaknesses, you can prepare yourselves to learn all that the Lord has for you in the experience of hardship. I can remember a morning when we were still trying to sort ourselves out after our debacle, when we suddenly understood: *There are two ways to respond to this experience. One is to withdraw, asking a whining, "Why?" and so shrivel in our souls. The other way is to reach out both hands for the experience . . . to "press against the pain" . . . to lean into the experience . . . and thus to learn all we can about this aspect of the human condition, and to grow.* We made up our minds that we would grow — no matter how it hurt. And Cam and I have found ourselves matured and quieted and corrected by the things we have faced together.

Of course, the days of hardship need not be ones of unbroken solemnity. In fact, heaven help the family who cannot laugh at themselves, laugh at their situation. (We do need to be careful here, for bitter laughter, laughter at each other's expense, and derisive laughter are all destructive. It is only the gentle laughter of people seeing life together, people who can see the ridiculousness of themselves or of their situation, that builds and helps.) The merciful gift of being able to laugh at ourselves — laugh with those we loved — was, for us, a healing agent.

Sharing the Load

Living on love means sharing the load. Sharing it in honest communication. Sharing it in recognition of individual strengths and honest acknowledgment of one another's failures. Sharing it in the assessment of lessons learned and new understandings gained. It also means sharing in the actual solution to the problem. It is not just enough to be honest with each other and then fold your hands and stare at the ceiling, waiting for a handout from the sky. God just does not work in that way. In fact, the New Testament is explicit about the necessity for working "with . . . [our] hands that [we] may have something to share with those in need" (Eph. 4:28).

Let me share with you a letter my mother wrote to her four children when she explained the terms of my grandfather's will. It tells a story of how a whole family shared the load.

Grandpa and Grandma Woods were very hardworking people with simple tastes and a contentment with their lot in life — always grateful to the Lord for His provision for them and their three children. Our home was furnished with plain, even rugged furniture, a few chintz cushions for the seats of the hardwood chairs being the only upholstery we knew. As we grew up and visited in the homes of our friends, we children began to see the new overstuffed Chesterfield suites which were really quite new on the market and we began to pester our parents for more elaborate things. Grandpa put a proposition to us: If we would help them save $1,000 as a cushion for emergencies first, they would then add some better furniture to our home. I would have been about ten or eleven years old, and my brothers were younger, so you realize the only way we could help was by not asking for things we didn't need.

We watched the bank account grow with real interest and did reach our goal. However, about the same time as we reached that goal, Grandpa lost his job with Canadian Pacific Railways because of the economic crash in 1929. He was able to get enough work that the emergency fund was not depleted, but even we children understood that luxuries were out. Then one day there was no more work to be obtained, and Grandpa decided to try creating his own job. With the $1,000 he set up a business, which God honored and prospered far beyond any expectation so that Grandpa was able to support and educate his family and provide jobs for his two sons when jobs were very difficult for young men to find. Grandpa never went into debt for anything either in business or in the home. If there was not cash to pay for things, we did without, but we never lacked any of the necessities of life and Grandpa was never on "relief" or welfare as we know it now. As long as we lived at home there was no new furniture but later, when things improved after World War II, Grandpa and Grandma did enjoy comforts which we today think are necessities.

Grandpa was generous in his giving to the Lord's work, and I cannot tell you how grateful I am to the Lord and to Grandpa and Grandma, not merely for the money in the estate, but for the godly heritage they have given us—the example of frugal living combined with a deep desire to obey God's Word at any cost.

There, of course, may be times when it is necessary for a Christian family to accept welfare or unemployment insurance. Sometimes there is no other choice. But as people of God we should normally do everything in our power to find ways to earn the bread we eat and to repay the debts we have incurred.

Solving the Most Pressing Problems

Obviously, when we face a job loss or a business failure, the immediate problem is finding money for the day-to-day needs of a family. We had to find enough for our family's ongoing needs and work out a way to pay back debts. Job-hunting may be challenging at the best of times, but it is made doubly difficult when the job-seeker is feeling crushed and damaged in self-esteem. Finding something to do to meet immediate needs will be, for most families as it was for us, the biggest single step toward recovery. It may mean taking jobs beneath normal expectations. It will probably mean assessing the mutual job-finding resources of an entire family, with several members finding part-time work to help out. The spouse with the more marketable skills will have to "go for it," with support tasks redistributed according to the number of hours spent outside the home in earning.

For us, the first provision of income was a half-time job teaching high school French—a job in my field, rather than Cam's. Cam did the housekeeping along with winding down the business while I crammed to brush up my rusty French and taught. By spring, with much of the business attended to, Cam was able to take a short-term teaching job in another nearby town. Now the children had to help out too. Cam's parents offered to look after our two preschoolers while I taught—another provision. When the little ones found it hard to interrupt their play and pack up for the daily drive into town, I would explain the situation to them: "We're all helping each other just now. Grandma and Grandpa are helping by looking after you. Mom and Dad are helping each other by teaching—and now you can help me by getting on your coats without complaining." And so they did.

And so our hard winter resolved itself into spring, with clothes and groceries and car gas being paid for as we went along. We were blessed in having teaching jobs available; today, with down-sizing in corporations and government cutbacks, many professional people are finding it impossible to get relocated within their own area of training. Had there been no teaching jobs available, however, we would have considered whatever other options presented themselves. We talked seriously about the possibility that Cam might have to take a laboring job in the far north, in oil or in construction. And he would have done that, had not a job opened up for him close at hand. When economic reversal hits, we cannot afford to consider ourselves "above" any type of employment, regardless of previous training or job. We knew that we would take work—any kind of work we could find—to prevent ourselves from going further backward. And at the same time, we pruned our already lean budget to fit within our earning power.

You probably remember the Aesop fable about the frog in the cream jug. As I remember it from a grade-school reader, it goes something like this:

> One day, a frog fell into a jug that had been set outside to cool. At first, as the cool thick liquid closed around him, the frog thought, "Alas, all is lost. I shall drown in this cream." But then the frog thought to himself: *If I am to drown, it is better to drown struggling than simply lying here and sinking like a rock.* And so the frog began to kick and struggle with all of his strength. At first the cream just flowed around him, and then, just when he thought he had no more strength left for the struggle, he felt a little clot behind a back leg, and, with just one more burst of energy, the frog was standing on a little pat of butter which had formed as he had churned. And from that pat of butter, the frog was able to make one last leap — out of the cream jug and back into the pond.

That's how we felt by the end of the twelve months of struggle in which we reorganized our business affairs and began life again. We were weary from the struggle, but strong . . . and out of the cream jug.

Chapter Five

Stopping the Merry-Go-Round

"Want it? Charge it!" It's as easy as that — and, for many of us, as complicated.

I see the credit card companies on the campus where I teach, university students being encouraged to "establish their credit rating" by getting a card, and I remember how seductive credit cards were for us. As young marrieds, we found credit cards to be the magic key that unlocked all the things that more established people had. By means of credit buying, we could start living almost at the level our parents had achieved after many years of careful accumulation. And so, like most young people, we applied for credit cards: gas company cards, department store cards, feeling like we were joining the Club.

We were cautious in the use of those cards. One of the first uses we made of them was to outfit our tiny teacherage with simple, basic furniture. We were certainly not spendthrift, buying everything on sale and choosing what we felt was the best compromise between price and quality that we could make. Thinking back on the sum of our various expenditures, the figure seems ludicrously small. The department store whose card we used delivered the furniture to our new home in the village where we taught, and the monthly statement began to arrive in our mailbox. We were part of the economy. We belonged!

And making the payments posed no problem, since we were both earning a regular paycheck. Nonetheless, I remember the feeling of discouragement when, month after month, we made our payments, and yet the balance owing seemed to stay so high. It was our first taste of the fact that it was much easier to charge than to pay.

We quit charging, all at once, when we decided to go back to study together. Instead of spending, we saved. And the interest, instead of adding onto a balance payable account, started to be added to our credit balance in our savings account. We banked one paycheck each month and lived and made our credit payment from the other. It was exhilarating to pull in our belts and save for a goal. Our student years were lean even with the help we received from my parents in reduced rent on a basement suite and from Cam's folks in farm-grown vegetables. (One friend commented that we knew more ways to cook turnips than any couple he knew.) But we finished our studies debt-free.

Probably even sadder than students getting their own credit cards before they have landed their first jobs is the debt many young people accumulate before ever getting to those jobs. The ball and chain of loan repayments that many young people have to drag through the first decade of employment makes me feel sad and angry. Angry that it is necessary for students to mortgage their futures for their education; sad that the standard of living for students has become so high that, for most students, extensive borrowing is the only way to sustain it. Especially with the uncertainty that there will be a job immediately upon graduation — at least a job commensurate with one's training and expectations — it might be better to "live lean." (OK, so skip the turnips! But, after all, learning frugality early may be the best part of an education for the years ahead!) Some should consider taking a year out from their studies to save ahead rather than incurring large student loans — loans which will have to be paid off at the low end of their earning power while they are trying to establish a home and start a family.

A New Start

With studies behind us for the time being, we celebrated life by making a down payment on a new car, buying a green canvas tent, and setting out on a cross-country camping trip. And then we entered consumer life in earnest. Cam was the principal of a school, and his income was about the same as our combined salaries had been prior to our return to the university. I was expecting our first child and had time to turn the pages of the fat catalogs which, for people in rural areas like ours, served as department stores. And, with my shiny new credit cards, I was able to charge the things we needed. I'm sure that everything I bought was quite legitimate and defensible. I know I never shopped frivolously. But I remember the sudden shock and panic that struck me when, after the delight of numbers of little parcels arriving in the mail, the statements followed. I could hardly imagine that the "few little things" I had bought had pushed the balance on our two accounts to a combined $300. The other shock came over the next few months. Do you know how long it takes to reduce a balance of $300 at the minimum monthly payment of $12? Forever. At least, it seems that long. Especially if you happen to add a thing or two to that account as you go along.

I was learning that the exciting consumer concept of revolving credit was a merry-go-round with the music stuck in an endless, mindless ditty of "buy now, and pay and pay and pay." It was a merry-go-round that never had to stop at all. And every ad I read, every page of every catalog, every visit to the department stores in the city, and every mailing "to preferred credit customers" was designed to flatter me with the idea that somehow I was a notch above the rest of the world because I held a red, white, or blue credit card for a given store.

Then we went farming. And when big spending times of the year came around—like snowsuit-time or Christmas—and there simply was no money because the grain was still not marketed, the charge cards came in handy again. I could rattle off those tempting numbers and, after dictating my order, say nonchalantly, "Just charge it to our account." I knew my numbers by heart. And I was treated with the deference given to regular charge customers. The balances began to build up again.

Worst of all, the monthly statements had a way of coming out to coincide with the time when most average people were bringing home their paychecks. But we had no paycheck. Just those big, tantalizing lump sums that came with shipping a load of pigs or selling a bin of grain—those big checks that melted away as we paid outstanding bills to the businesses that had delivered our gas, stockpiled our fertilizer, or sold us seed. It was hard to scratch up enough, on a month-to-month basis, to pay even the minimum payments on those charge accounts. And if there's one thing I cannot face, it's a dunner: "We hope that your failure to make a payment last month was an oversight. However, terms of our credit agreement with you stipulate that if we do not receive your payment of ＿＿＿＿＿＿＿ by ＿＿＿＿＿＿, we shall ＿＿＿＿＿＿." Those notes devastated me. Not that we were defaulting in any long-term way. As soon as there was money, we paid the back payment and one or two in advance. We simply limped from lump to lump. And between times, I would find myself having to charge something or other, pushing up that balance once again.

It finally dawned on me that the whole principle of the revolving credit system was that you should never get a balance paid off. You should always have a balance, pay interest on it, pay off some and add on some. And about the same time, it dawned on me that it was those monthly accounts that made me most unhappy and most discontent. They were the things that precipitated those "Why can't we live like normal people?" discussions with Cam which cheered him so. Combining each month—with fiendish regularity—with those days when I felt mad at the world in general—those bills made month ends very blue.

Taking Charge
One year I finally made the big decision: there was no way that I was going to charge one thing for Christmas. Not one little thing. Cam and I liked to have great Christmas gifts for the kids. But when we noticed that we were still paying for each

Christmas deep into the following year, we made our decision firm. "No matter how little we can buy, we're going to pay cash for Christmas gifts this year." Now, that may sound only reasonable to you, but for us it was a new departure, a new beginning. We paid cash for Christmas, trimming the gift list, withdrawing from drawing names, and shopping as thriftily as we could. And on that Christmas Day, every gift that was opened was prepaid. The only day nicer than December 25 was January 25, when there were no additional charges on those revolving accounts of ours. And February 25. And March 25. Less pressure, less depression, fewer arguments.

That experiment prepared us to take action when several years later, we found that our cattle-feeding company was completely broke. We took what little money we had in the bank and paid all of our charge accounts: gas accounts, department store accounts, and the grocery account. It left us flat. But from that day we decided that during this time of financial exigency, either the Lord would supply us with cash or we would not buy. That applied right down to the next loaf of bread we needed for school lunches. We learned to pray, "Give us this day our daily bread." And He did. There was often very little extra. Cam used to say, "You know, our cupboards would make Mother Hubbard's look like a supermarket." But there was always enough—for that day, at least.

I remember well a week when all our food supplies were at an all-time low. But we had no money. None at all. So we took our request to the Lord in prayer. The last day of the week, the mail contained two small checks: one a reprint fee for an article of mine, the other a small overpayment refund for Cam. The total was no staggering amount, but we went shopping. We shopped with all the joy I used to know as a little girl with a dime to spend in Woolworth's. We shopped selectively. We picked things up, adding up the total in our heads as we went, and then pushed the cart back and returned some of the things to the shelves. And when we went home, we had all that we needed. Plus joy and gratitude.

The greatest delight, besides that of having no more month-end pressures when month ends brought so little of anything else, was the pleasure of being freed from the need to buy. I could look at one of those ads reading, "Go Ahead! Charge It!" and feel more nausea than desire. I had the happy feeling that month by month, despite inflation, I was at least not having to pay those scarcely perceptible little service charges and exorbitant interest rates that are normal on credit-card accounts.

I noticed something else too. Without those credit cards in my purse, I was free to shop. I mean, really shop. I didn't have to go to the stores where I was a gilt-edged, card-carrying member. I could go anywhere for the best values. I noticed it most of all when buying gas. As long as I had a particular company's card in my purse, all I looked for was a service station sporting the right color and shape of sign, and wheeled in for gas. Without those little bits of plastic, I read, instead, the price-per-gallon signs, and bought where the price was right.

Getting off the credit merry-go-round was just part of our overall "face-the-facts" policy. Not that using a charge card is wrong for everyone. Many people are able to control their spending well enough to pay every credit balance in full. But allowing yourself to buy things you cannot afford today, in the hope that you will be able to afford them—plus interest—next month, is living a myth. So is it when you think that buying things in easy monthly payments is really easy. It's not. Without those plastic crutches, I could look at our bank balance and decide whether I could afford to buy or not. Some years, it has been mostly not. And yet, the goodness of the Lord's provision is unforgettable.

Steps to Controlled Credit

If you are on the credit-card trip and want to get off, here are some tips. First of all, in order to get the charge accounts paid, you need to impose a period of several months of real austerity on yourself, buying only absolute necessities like groceries. If you have a regular income, budget to pay off the accounts in an orderly way as fast as you can. And put nothing—but nothing—more on that account. "I can hardly wait," a friend of mine told me. "In a couple of months, we should have all our accounts paid off. Then we're going to only buy with cash." And then she went to the city with her charge cards in her purse. The temptation was too much as she browsed in the big stores. "It all came to only $250," she told me as she showed me her purchases. "I charged it." Six months later we each drank a Coke as we chatted. "That miserable charge account is right up there again," she sighed. "And it all started that time I charged those clothes."

The way to stop the merry-go-round is to put those credit cards in some safe and nonpilferable place—anywhere but your purse. If you do not want to destroy them yet, store them in an envelope, deep in a file, or better yet, in a safety deposit box. That will make them hard to grab when your fingers get the dial-an-order itch. If you must make purchases while you are trying to reduce your charge accounts, pay cash. And chisel away at the balances you owe as fast as you can. Then, when the accounts are down to a zero balance and you get that lovely letter, reading, "We are pleased with the excellent way in which you have handled your credit. Please feel free to use your credit card at any time"—and the follow-up one which tells you what a valued customer you are and how they yearn to send you a bill once more—forget it. It's not real love.

Living in the Real World
Now, at last, you can begin to live in the real world. And despite all the invitations to use credit as though money will somehow "happen along" later, we all know that everyone, from governments to individuals, has to face reentry into the reality of economics: for goods received, value must be given. And the easiest, surest, most direct way to be sure that you can give value for goods received is to pay as you go—an idea so old-fashioned as to be positively avant-garde.

Living in this real world, you will exercise restraint, and begin the lifelong learning process of disciplining your heart to contentment. As you learn how to distinguish between wants and needs, you will no longer be driven by advertising. "And my God will meet all your needs" is God's promise to His children, backed by "His glorious riches in Christ Jesus" (Phil. 4:19). But nowhere, *not anywhere,* in Scripture does God invite us to help ourselves to everything we want. In fact, we are continually warned to beware of buying into a value system that is driven by "the cravings of sinful man, the lust of his [or her] eyes and the boasting of what he [or she] has and does" (1 John 2:16). You might try analyzing the advertisements in a current magazine or on an evening of television by those three motivational phrases. They still represent the fundamental drives behind our desire to buy and consume beyond our real needs. Isn't that why advertisers pay huge sums to TV networks and big money to clever makers of commercials — to get you to buy?

In our lean years, I learned a way I still use to winnow out "needs" from "wants." Once in awhile, I make a list of all the things that I would like to have that are badgering away at my brain — usually on a back page of the coil notebook I call my "journal." Just getting them out of my head and onto paper helps clear my head. Often I can immediately distinguish between bubbles, baubles, and needs. A few days later many of the items on it do not seem quite so pressing as they did when I wrote them down. Now I can quite deliberately separate the items into several lists: In "List A" I can place items which fulfill physical needs — clothes suitable to the climate in which we live; warm and adequate housing; nutritious food for ourselves and our families; some mode of transportation — an essential need unless you live where public transportation can get you where you have to go. In "List B" I prioritize items which fulfill social needs — like gifts to be purchased or supplies for a celebration. In "List C" I can list items which are related to production: from the tape recorder or word processor that would help me get my work done to the combine we need to buy for farming. Items which do not fit into any of these lists, I can relegate to "List D" — a wish list of "someday-maybe" things which are attractive and legitimate but not essential at this time.

"List A" items are top priority items — needs to be met as soon as and to the extent that we can afford. "List B" items may have to be scaled down to fit the budget — but they too need to be looked after. "List C" items are business decisions which need to be looked at in terms of productive capability. If they will not directly affect production, they will have to wait for cash on hand; if they will really increase earning capability, they may be capital expenditures necessary to getting on with our work, something we might have to arrange a short-term loan for.

"List D" items — the "someday-maybe" ones — tend to lose their urgency when they get separated from more pressing needs. I can look at them and ask some other questions, like, "Is this an item that I might want to put in a garage sale a few years from now?"

I can now go back through those lists and number them in order of priority — and on the basis of that, make wise spending decisions.

Using Credit Wisely

I have been talking about getting off the endless merry-go-round of credit for consumable items. There are, of course, other kinds of completely legitimate credit which I am sure God intends for Christians to use wisely and well. Very few families could have a home if they had to pay cash for it. Very few could start a business. And most people would not even be able to drive a car. Christian thinkers have drawn a distinction between borrowing for consumable items (debt) and borrowing for capital items (investment). This difference is set forth memorably in Robert Schuller's account of how his banker explained to him the meaning of debt:

> When you borrow money for coal, you are going into debt. The coal will be burned. When it is gone, if you are unable to pay your loan, there is nothing you can sell to pay us back. When you borrow money for coal,

or food, or the light bill, or the water bill, you are spending money that is gone forever. This is real debt.

But the banker went on to explain:

> If you want to borrow money to buy a car or a house, we will lend you money. Then you are not going into debt; you are going into the investment business. . . . If you borrow money to buy a store and you borrow money for salable goods to put on the shelves, you are not in debt. You are in business.[1]

Yet, here again, a clear head, an open Bible, a good banker, and a clear line of communication between you and your mate are necessary to be sure that you are using credit instead of it using you. In our farming company, the money we borrowed was very legitimate and used for the purposes of production. Yet, we still borrowed ourselves into very serious economic problems. An article in *Changing Times,* the Kiplinger Magazine, suggests "one safety rule is never to owe more at any one time than you can repay within twelve months at your current rate of payments," making, of course, exceptions for large, long-term loans such as those for homes.[2] Another rule of thumb would be never to borrow more than you have fixed assets to cover. Thus, if you found yourself unable to meet current obligations, you would be able to sell assets and cover your indebtedness.

Friends of ours recently recounted to us that when their insurance agent came to review their coverage, they decided to have him help them draw up a net worth statement. They listed all of their assets in one column, and totaled them; all of their liabilities were listed in a second column and totaled. When the insurance man subtracted the total liabilities from their total assets, he looked up at them, obviously surprised. They had a substantial surplus of assets. "You know," the insurance salesman told them, "there are very few couples today who have a positive net worth. When I work this out for most people, we find they actually owe more than they own."

When You Cannot Pay

Another problem remains to be discussed in this credit-abundant society. What about credit debts which you have at the moment that your business goes sour? Or you lose your job? Or illness destroys your earning power while adding burdens?

A Christian cannot just walk away from debt. His word is pledged, and he must acknowledge his obligations. But to avoid an unpleasant outcome, the best route is simply to be honest and open. Go to your creditors personally, or write them a letter. Explain the situation and ask for time in which to reorganize your finances. Suggest a time when you will be able to begin to reduce the debt, if that time can be foreseen. Let them know your fiscal condition, and assure them that you are serious about repaying the obligation. If you are straightforward and honest, if you have pared down your lifestyle to an extremely modest standard so that you are credible, if you continue to keep in touch and make even token payments of good faith, then your creditors will be remarkably patient as you attempt to get your business affairs straightened out.

I once worked as a typist in collection agencies. In one office, I typed envelopes while at ten or twelve desks in the same large room men sat and dialed persons whose debts were considered "bad" and had been turned over to them for collection. The men yelled and threatened and bullied, and I felt the horror of how it must feel to be at the other end of such a call. But creditors do not like turning accounts over to collection agencies, since they lose a percentage of every payment collected. Despite financial problems, we have found that honesty with our creditors, restraint in our personal living, and systematic planning for repayment of what seemed to us to be staggering debts have resulted in fair and courteous treatment from those to whom we have owed money. We rejected bankruptcy as a means of avoiding debt obligations, even though our debts had been incurred by a limited company. And, through the goodness of the Lord and the patience of our creditors, we have been able to pay back all that we owed. It is a good feeling—a mixture of gratitude and relief.

So, do we still use credit? Yes, of course. But very cautiously, never forgetting the sick feeling of finding debt out of control. We do use credit cards to avoid having to carry around a lot of cash, but we are still aware of how easy it is to overspend with plastic. Paying the full balance every month keeps us from getting back on the buy-now and pay-forever merry-go-round we remember too well. Our businesses run on operating credit which allows us to seed a crop in the spring and harvest it in the fall, or take time off from my teaching or speaking to write a book, and yet keep a relatively stable cash flow. And although we have retired much of our capitalization debt, we are still making payments on long-term loans for land and machinery.

We remember now how, on our honeymoon, we went with friends to an exhibition ground where we went through the exhilaration and terror of the enormous roller coaster, bounced on the trampolines, and survived some other rides. Then we all went out together for Alka-Seltzer. That's how the memory of overextended credit feels to us; we're a bit squeamish, even yet; we get sick at the thought of it ever getting out of control. But we are off the roller coaster, for good.

Chapter Six

Basic Needs I: Sharing the Good Things

We are not a family big on playing board games. Not that there is anything wrong with them; we have admired families that have made more time for game-playing. Maybe our lack of interest has been because life itself has sometimes seemed like a complicated and frustrating enough board game. I remember how, in the midst of our financial reversal, I could not stand playing games where some flick of the wrist might mean you got a message: "Return to Start." We were in the process of doing that, and it was no fun. Or maybe our lack of interest in games is because, when we get together with others, we would rather have a conversation than total up points. Or maybe it is nothing more or less than pure pragmatics: as a family we found other means of entertainment simply because we could not afford to purchase every new game that came along. At any rate, we have a sparse collection of games in our games cupboard.

But although our choice of games was not big, we did develop a tradition: at least once during the Christmas holidays, we would sit down and play a game of Monopoly with Mitchell, our youngest son, who had already demonstrated his entrepreneurial instincts by the time he was six and was caring for the seven little weanling pigs his sow had birthed. He still remembers (with some vexation) how I used to lay aside 10 percent of any payout I received and play it on a second, imaginary game board on which I could buy food for hungry kids, place Bibles in people's hands in their own languages, develop literacy and agricultural programs, and support missionaries in church-planting. And when the end of the game came (admittedly, a bit sooner than it might have had I not pulled so much play money out of circulation), I usually not only owned Park Avenue but also had made an imagined difference somewhere, in someone's life.

Playing Monopoly so subversively was a lighthearted but natural way in which to express one of our fundamental beliefs: the conviction that giving is not something one does once in awhile, but a basic need, something that we do as a part of our economic existence.

The Need to Give

No matter how hard-pressed we have been, we have found that one of our first and most basic needs is the need to share in the "shalom" or well-being of others. Since from our Christian perspective, that well-being is complex and includes the physical, emotional, intellectual, and spiritual needs of others, the range of ways in which we are able to give is also wide and complex. In concentric circles of caring, beginning with our own family circle and widening out to our church family and community and then to the larger community, we have tried to keep aware of others as well as of our own needs.

Our gifts of money have been, as such have always been seen to be, earthly tokens of an essentially spiritual commitment: our lives themselves are gifts from God; all that we have and are we have given — or are in the daily process of learning how to give — back to the Giver. Monetary gifts remind us of that underlying commitment. And, as C.S. Lewis puts it, "If our charities do not at all pinch or hamper us, I should say they are too small."[1]

Because giving meets two basic needs in our own lives — our need to affirm "who we are" by reminding ourselves of "whose we are" as well as our need to live in connection with other needy human beings in order to keep our own needs in perspective—we have found it works best to plan our giving and do it first. Whenever we have tried to save a little throughout the month in order to give, we have found that our own needs have overwhelmed our urge to give. But when we have given our love-gifts first, we have found that somehow there has been enough for the month ahead. I am not sure that I know *how* that works—but I know *that* it works.

Biblical Principles of Giving

Giving as a basic mark of discipleship is stressed throughout the New Testament. Jesus looked out at a hungry crowd and laid the responsibility for the welfare of the people directly on the shoulders of His disciples—the very people who had given up their means of earning a living to follow Him: "You give them something to eat" (Matt. 14:16). The disciples were, apparently, stunned at the command. They did the mental calculations and felt their empty purses. And they learned that, if they were to fulfill their Lord's command, they would have to rely on their Lord's resources.

Paul continues the theme of openhanded giving, inviting the Christian believers at Philippi to give not only to meet his needs, but to meet their own need of obedient giving. (You can follow his discussion of this important theme in Philippians 4:10-20.) Giving, Paul argues, produces lasting spiritual benefit in the lives of the givers.

Of course, giving is not a novel theme in the New Testament. It is simply an enlargement of a theme already developed in the Old Testament. Because God is love, throughout history those who have understood His revelation of Himself have understood the obligation of sharing the good things of life with others. The tradition of giving as a moral responsibility can be traced back as far as to Job. In defending his righteous conduct, Job recounts acts of charity which he sees to be both social and spiritual obligations:

If I have denied the desires of the poor or let the eyes
    of the widow grow weary,

if I have kept my bread to myself,
   not sharing it with the fatherless. . . .
if I have seen anyone perishing for
   lack of clothing,
   or a needy man without a garment,
and his heart did not bless me
   for warming him with the fleece from my sheep
. . . then let my arm fall from the shoulder,
   let it be broken off at the joint.
For I dreaded destruction from God,
   and for fear of His splendor I could not do
   such things (Job 31:16-23).

Job's sense of social obligation is rooted in his fear of the Lord: his sense that he lives out his life in the presence of One whose holiness demands that His creatures take responsibility for each other.

Yet, Job was still yearning for "Someone" to come: "If only there were someone to arbitrate between us, to lay his hand upon us both, someone to remove God's rod from me" (Job 9:33-34). That "Someone" has come in the person of the Lord Jesus Christ. The New Testament believer, motivated by love for the One who "though He was rich, yet for [our] sakes He became poor, so that [we] through His poverty might become rich" (2 Cor. 8:9) should surely not be less socially responsible than was Job. In glad and loving response to Jesus' self-giving, we *need* to give.

We need to give, and not only because there are physical needs which must be met by our giving. Our "headline news" awareness of those needs make us painfully aware of them, so painfully aware, in fact, that sometimes we become anesthetized, inured by visual familiarity to so much suffering. We need to give also because in giving we share in "the grace of our Lord Jesus Christ." In giving, in sharing in His gracious self-giving, we begin to learn a little of what it is to be Christlike — the lifetime goal of any believer. After all, the One who Jesus invites us to call "Father" is, at heart, the Great Giver (as

Jesus teaches in Matthew 5:43-48, and James reiterates in James 1:16-18).

And as *forgiving others* seems to be necessary to clear a channel through which God's forgiveness can reach us (Matt. 6:14-15), so *giving to others* seems to operate to clear a channel through which we can receive God's physical provision for our needs. It is not that we give more in order to receive more — but that we give something in order to open the way for the provision of "our daily bread." We do not give away the money the Lord has given us for our mortgage payment and expect to get double the amount in the mail the next day. We budget our incomes and discipline ourselves to give, proportionate to what God entrusts to us for our stewardship, in accordance with clear New Testament principles and guidelines. These principles cover matters of *motivation* for giving, the *measure* of our giving, and the *method* of our giving.

1. *Motivation.* The motivation of love and obedience that prompts Christian giving will always be a mystery to those on the outside looking in. No matter how sophisticated and professional our fund-raising appeals may become, the secret of lifelong generous giving that combines discipline with joy will always be found, as it was in the generous, poverty-stricken Christians of the opening decades of the history of the church, in people's giving of themselves "first to the Lord and then to [others]" (2 Cor. 8:1-5). Other appeals — whether based on sentimental response to the pathos of others' needs or on the very human desire to be part of some spectacular project or program may result in spasms of philanthropy, but will never produce steady, sustained giving.

The motivation for Christian "charity" is not primarily in the need of others — although the Christian is aware of those needs and seeks to meet them. Even less is it in any idea that God needs our gifts in order to accomplish His will. We do not give because God needs our money. We give because He invites us to share in His goodness. We give because we live in relationship with a God who is a Giver. We give because in giving we grow in our capacity to know and love Him. We give because giving is the natural, glad response of love and thanksgiving for God's goodness to us. We are not primarily motivated by the needs we see, real and pressing as they are. Rather, we first decide to give out of love to God, and then we find the needs that our gifts might best address.

There have been times when we have been able to give more, and times when we have been able to give less. There have been times when we could give with the delight of skimming cream off the rich milk of God's goodness, and times when the milk was so thin it was blue — and we offered from our skim milk. We have been assured from Scripture that God was pleased to accept and bless our gifts, whether they came from our prosperity or from our poverty.

2. *Measure.* How much should we give? These days, in a reaction against legalism, we are in danger of losing touch with our deep traditions and history. The church for centuries held out the measure or norm of the tithe: one-tenth of all that is entrusted to us is to be returned to God as a matter of course.

And in doing that, the church was simply extending a deep and ancient practice from the Old Testament. By the end of the Old Testament, the tithe was so clearly understood as a principle that to withhold it could be declared to be a form of theft. In the dialogue between God and His people in the Book of Malachi, God asks: "Will a man rob God? Yet you rob Me." The people of God reply, "How do we rob You?" And God's answer is clear: "In tithes and offerings" (Mal. 3:7-8). If the tithe was an appropriate standard of giving for the Old Testament, the New Testament standard would surely be to give at least as much as the tithe — surely not less than the tithe. Jesus, fulfilling the spirit of the Old Testament Law in His relationship with God and with others, sets the standard of total giving in His self-emptying.

For me, the tithe continues to make sense as the foundational principle of systematic giving. It seems to me to be a principle which, since it was clearly practiced long before the giving of the Mosaic Law, is still "in force" now, after the fulfillment of the Mosaic Law by our Lord Jesus Christ. Abraham, we read, tithed to Melchizedek, king and priest (as reported in Genesis 14:18 and commented on in Hebrews 7). Abraham seems to have tithed not because tithing was a law, but apparently because it was a principle of giving that had already been established by tradition. We, who claim "faithful Abraham" as a spiritual ancestor, should surely give as faithfully in the name of and for the advancement of the kingdom of our High Priest and King, Jesus Christ.

Jacob is another of the patriarchs who demonstrates that tithing is not just a rule of law. He made a business deal with God:

> If God will be with me and will watch over me on this journey I am taking and will give me food to eat and clothes to wear so that I return safely to my father's house, then the Lord will be my God . . . and of all that You give me I will give You a tenth (Gen. 28:20-22).

And even though the cheating, self-interested Jacob still had a long way to go before he would return to that place of covenant to be renamed (Gen. 35:9), the deal he made reinforces the point that the tithe is not just some sort of legal obligation, but deeply rooted in a tradition. *The tithe is paid by those who live out their lives by faith in an unseen God.*

So it seems to me that it is quite compatible with Scripture to see the tithe as the basic unit of giving — rooted in pre-Mosaic Law relationships of God and His people, a standard by which giving less than the tithe is judged to be simple robbery, and a principle echoed in the New Testament in the principle of proportional giving. "On the first day of every week, each one of you should set aside a sum of money *in keeping with his [or her] income*" (1 Cor. 16:2, emphasis added). Returning to God 10 percent of the total income that has been entrusted to us is a way to be sure that our giving is proportional to our prosperity.

If tithing is the foundational principle of giving — the floor under our giving — then we might consider that, as my father used to put it, "Giving starts where tithing leaves off." And I can remember an envelope on my parents' dresser ready for the offering labeled with my father's precise cursive—"Lord's Money." That envelope was the first thing attended to when the monthly paycheck came. Everything else came after that.

Giving, then, represents digging a bit deeper or reaching a bit higher. For some in extreme duress, the tithe may be all that can be returned to the Lord. For others, the tithe will be a small portion of what can be spared. For people who carry a heavy debt load, a matter of integrity is involved. After they have tithed, they must give primary attention to the repaying of contracted obligations. God cannot be honored by Christians who default on debts or postpone repayment in order to respond to some need. (And, by the way, that's just one more good reason to keep off the credit merry-go-round. If you don't have those monthly statements to pay, you may be able to cinch in your belt and give generously to a need that the Lord brings to your attention.) I find most challenging a concept of "needs limitation" in which Christian families accept a fixed figure at which they can live simply and modestly but without undue pressure. They adjust that figure to the annual rise in the cost of living, and then, rather than expanding their needs to meet their income, they expand their giving to invest the balance of their income for the glory of God. All income over and above the fixed ceiling can be given to the Lord. Another interesting idea is Ronald J. Sider's modest proposal for a graduated tithe. He says in an article in *Theology, News and Notes:*

> How about a graduated or sliding scale for our giving? We could sit down and carefully and honestly figure out what we would need to live for a year in reasonable comfort, but without some of the luxuries . . . plus a certain amount for each child. . . . We would give a tithe on the basic amount. . . . Then, on the first $1,000 over the basic amount, we would give 15 percent to the Lord's work; on the next $1,000, we would give 20 percent.[2]

And so on. It's another workable plan for people who are serious about giving by God's standard.

3. *Method.* So, you've got your tithes and offerings figured out. Or you have written the amount on a check. Now, just to whom should you make that amount payable? It would be simple, wouldn't it, if we could just write "God" on the payable line and let Him take it from there. But God uses earthly clearinghouses. And the responsibility of stewardship comes into the picture again. God does not rule out our intelligence or our responsibility when it comes to giving. No merit exists in mindless, purposeless giving of our tithes and offerings as we are blown about by every breeze of fervent appeal.

We need to give systematically, prayerfully, and thoughtfully if we are to be considered faithful stewards. There are three main areas to which our giving will be directed under the leading of the Holy Spirit and the teaching of the Word of God:

• *Our local church.* Every local fellowship of believers has material obligations which require its support. The first concern is paying the pastor: "Anyone who receives instruction in the Word must share all good things with his instructor" (Gal. 6:6). The gaunt and starving preacher should exist only among gaunt and starving people. God's Word is clear about the responsibility of God's people to attend carefully to the physical needs of the one who labors for their spiritual benefit. A minister should live at the average standard of living of his parishioners, neither higher nor lower. If all tithes (as distinct from offerings) were given to the local church, and half of them were used to support the general church budget, building maintenance, and programs, the other half of the tithes of every twenty families could support a minister at a wage representing an exact average of their incomes. It is something to think about, although simplistic, perhaps, in terms of large churches with huge buildings, many staff members, and multitudinous programs. Yet the principle remains: a lion's share of our giving, at least of our tithing, needs to be channeled into supporting our local church. As a pastor of mine once put it: "You pay for your groceries at the store where you buy them—not at some other store down the street. So with your giving. You give your tithes where you and your family are getting the bread of life." If you find yourself unable to support the programs and ministries of the church you attend with your tithes, perhaps you should look for another fellowship whose message or method you can endorse more wholeheartedly, and to which you can give not only your time but also your tithe.

• *Giving to further the proclamation of the Gospel.* This involves looking out beyond the local, community programs of your own church, and seeing the need for worldwide evangelism. It should be a priority item on every Christian's "gift list." If your church or denomination has a strong missionary program, you may direct your gifts through that channel. You might also like to save some of your offerings for more personal giving. Many missionaries are proclaiming the Gospel of Jesus Christ while being supported solely by the monthly gifts of friends at home. And when you know such a "faith missionary" personally, or feel moved by the Spirit of God to support the work of one, you will experience that rare kind of joy that comes from many years of participation—by prayer and gifts—in another's ministry.

To me the most important aspect of this kind of sharing is that it helps you to remember that missionary friend on a regular basis. Your giving has a face on it. And, as Jesus pointed out, "Where your treasure is, there will your heart be also" (Matt. 6:21). The partnership which begins with giving matures into a prayer fellowship which means that you enter personally into the work of evangelism. Thus, even though your share of a missionary's support may be miniscule, those few dollars a month represent an investment of yourself in the missionary's work. Your family can join in the excitement of letters exchanged and furlough-time visits, and all of you will be enriched by this kind of fellowship.

Another kind of special love relationship is in supporting an indigenous pastor or evangelist. Here, there is a multiplication of your dollars in supporting people who already know the languages and cultures in which they seek to work, and whose monetary needs are much lower than even the most frugal North American.

• *Physical needs of the hungry and suffering.* This is a third kind of need to which Christian giving is directed. Giving to relieve the hungry, the destitute, the victims of catastrophe should not supplant our giving to the local church or to the cause of world evangelism. But in these days we should be giving more, over and above our tithes and regular offerings whenever possible, as we recognize our responsibility to relieve human suffering wherever we can. There are excellent Christ-centered and love-motivated organizations handling relief funds skillfully that we can give to in the loving Spirit of Christ.

Day after day, as we flip the pages of our magazines and turn on our television sets, we find ourselves looking into the eyes of hunger-haunted little ones, children of poverty, children of disease. And the ache becomes so great that we have to anesthetize ourselves. Or respond. Jesus' story of the sheep and goats in the great Judgment Day should be reread and restudied for its social implications today (Matt. 25:31-46). We will, as nations, be judged for our generosity—or lack of it—to those in need. And if as nations, then surely as individuals we will have to give account for our responsiveness. Some of us will have much to give; some, very little. But all of us can give, remembering that God measures our giving not in terms of how much we give, but rather, in terms of how much we keep for ourselves.

John Wesley, pondering the dilemma of the link between righteousness and riches, made a suggestion which is still valid today:

> Is there no way to prevent this continued decay of pure religion? We ought not to prevent people from being diligent and frugal; we must exhort all Christians to gain all they can and save all they can, that is, in effect, to grow rich. What way can we take that our money-

making may not sink us to the nethermost hell? There is one way. . . . *If those who gain all they can and save all they can will also give all they can, then, the more they will grow in grace and the more treasure they will lay up in heaven.*"[3]

Chapter Seven

Basic Needs II: Food and Clothing

Food

In the midst of our financial stress, I had a long period of illness leading up to major surgery. As I lay in a hospital bed watching the drip of the intravenous tube, I thought about how much time I would save in my life if we all just ate intravenously all the time. Just think, no time spent in food preparation or clean-up. I could just sit at my typewriter all day, every day, and eat through my hand! Of course, the idea was ludicrous. For food is very much a part of our lives, and you have to be pretty sick before another arrangement for nourishment looks better than sitting down together to a meal.

In personal spending, food takes one of the major chunks of our income — in North America, something between 18 and 25 percent of disposable income, depending on the level of income. Of course, in many countries of the world, the percentage of earned income spent on food is much higher — in some countries, people have to spend up to 80 percent of what is earned just to eat.[1]

And in daily living, as any homemaker knows, food demands a good deal of our time and attention. Growing it, shopping for it, storing it, preparing it, serving it, cleaning up after it: it all takes time.

There's nothing wrong with that, of course. But anything that demands such a large part of our income and our daily energy surely needs to be thought through carefully. We need to have healthy, sane attitudes toward food so that we can be good custodians of our food dollars, of the time we spend on, with, and over food, and ultimately, of the bodies we are responsible for nurturing.

Nutrition and Celebration

Food, of course, is more than merely a matter of nutrition — although that is its primary significance. We eat in order to live, and the nutritional role of food in the shaping of healthy bodies and minds is a matter of such importance that we really cannot just leave it to chance. We need to be informed and knowledgeable about food and nutrition.

But, over and above nutrition, food serves a secondary but also important role in our lives as an element of celebration. Our need for nutrition is undeniable; it is a physical requisite. But our need for celebration is an emotional, social, and spiritual aspect of life which we cannot neglect, either. And food serves as a center or focal point of celebration not only at special festive seasons — Thanksgiving, Christmas, Easter in our Western Christian tradition — but also daily as we gather as families for a shared meal, celebrating the provision of "our daily bread."

It seems a particularly perverse turn of events that in our Western societies, with access to great quantities of food, we should have lost sight of the value of food in both of its aspects: so many of our meals are haphazard events, taken hastily and with little planning from package to plate and eaten while plumped in individualized isolation in front of the television.

A period of real hardship probably had the beneficial effect for us of making us really notice what we had always before taken for granted: The gift of provision on a daily basis as a gift to be celebrated together. I can remember the joy we shared together in churning butter in a glass "Daisy churn," the children taking turns as the wooden paddles at first moved easily in the milk and then gradually became harder and harder to turn. Cam usually had to take over before we reached the exciting "voilà" moment when, suddenly, we had butter. I remember too the joy of receiving a small check for an article in the mail just in time for Saturday shopping.

I especially remember a Saturday when we had company coming for supper. We had home-churned butter for our home-baked bread. We had home-grown beef and home-hoed potatoes. But what could we have for dessert? Sugar prices had soared that winter as our income had plummeted, and I was eking out a five-pound bag by teaspoonfuls. As a family, we had quit having desserts with regular meals. But as I selected a few groceries at the village store, I glanced up to see the proprietor's wife blocking my way, holding a big bag of oranges. "Could you use these?" she asked. "They won't keep over the weekend." Sliced oranges, topped with fresh whipped cream, made our dessert that night. Our guests were charmed: such simplicity! such originality!

Blessedly, we had four little children to keep our mealtimes celebratory — sometimes uproariously so. We needed the buoyancy and joy of the children, and fed on their laughter and chatter and sense of the ridiculous even as they fed on the food we had prepared. For us, the evening meal each day became a central celebration of life and of each other.

I am not, of course, suggesting that every evening meal looked like one of those mouth-watering illustrations in the women's magazines. Stew or homemade soup and a thousand variations on hamburger casseroles and skillets were staples. Nor am I suggesting that every supper was an idyll of family sweetness and light. We had lots of salt and vinegar in our relationships too. But meals were planned; and we did sit down together to eat them. And after the food had disappeared into six healthy appetites, we asked for another disappearing act: We told the kids to go find things to do and Cam and I instituted our own private celebration — time to talk, just the two of us, over a shared pot of tea, with the noise of the children in the background.

Making Good Food Choices
Probably because food preparation does not "come naturally" to me, because the office rather than the kitchen is the room

in which I feel most competent and at home, I have always had to *think* about nutrition. And because I have at various times been very short of dollars, I have had to really *think* about value too.

To confirm and correct some of my own hunches about making good food choices, especially when on a stringently limited budget, I met with Dr. Deanna Swinamer, a young doctor who has not only her M.D. but also a B.Sc. in nutrition and a M.Sc. in experimental medicine. She is a registered dietician as well as a family physician. Dr. Swinamer stressed that people do not need to buy special products in order to be healthy—but they do need to learn to think intelligently about food.

We talked about making good choices in the various food groups areas. About *fat*, Dr. Swinamer says, "It's a lot more important just to cut down on fat in general, always choosing lower fat foods, for instance, than to know the difference between polyunsaturated and saturated fats," she says. "In general, the North American diet has too much fat in it—so watch for the lower milk fat (M.F.) or butter fat (B.F.) figures on products like cheese and yogurt. There is no need for fanaticism—small quantities of fat won't hurt you. But just make a general rule of using less fat, choosing lower fat products."

Dr. Swinamer likes to use broth for sautéing vegetables rather than fat, and suggests that it be bought dehydrated in bulk to serve as a base for stir fries or fried rice. What about peanut butter, every mother's best friend? It is inexpensive and can be counted on to be a favorite with most children. "Peanut butter is fine," Dr. Swinamer says. "If I were a mother of young kids, would I buy a big can of generic-brand peanut butter? You bet I would. It's good nutrition, especially if combined with mashed banana. But why not just hold the margarine or butter, so you are not doubling up on the fat content of a sandwich?"

Protein, Dr. Swinamer says, "has taken a beating. But we need protein—and for most people, red meat is needed in the diet. Our bodies do not store protein, so daily intake is necessary. It's especially important for adolescent girls who are unlikely to get adequate iron and protein from other sources," she says. "If people would just buy lean beef and pork and remember that a recommended serving size of three ounces is much smaller than most people realize, they could eat meat without worrying about it."

She recommends using "meat stretchers" — smaller amounts of meat are needed in a casserole dinner than when served alone. Tinned tuna or salmon can be mixed with mayonnaise and yogurt for a nutritious spread on whole wheat bread or bagels. (Actually, I had an elderly woman describe to me the greatest meat stretcher I ever heard of: she called it "Potato and Point.")

> "We were so poor when I was a child on the east coast," she told me, "that we used to have what we called 'potato and point.' We would cook a tiny portion of meat, usually pork, and the fragrance of that meat would fill the whole house with a wonderful smell. And then my mother would suspend that little piece of meat over the table where we could all enjoy its aroma and serve us the usual huge pot of potatoes. With each bite, we would point our forks toward the meat and imagine its flavor, and then eat our potatoes with the taste of salt pork." (Now, that's stretching it!)

There are, of course, vegetable sources of protein that should be added into our diets: Peas and lentils and a whole range of beans provide cheap and excellent protein sources, better known in some other cultures than in traditional North American food patterns. We are beginning to learn from Mexican and other Hispanic people how to use these sources of protein, both as meat-stretchers and as meat-replacers in our diets.

Carbohydrates, Dr. Swinamer suggests, can be provided inexpensively in a whole range of ways. Pasta is wonderful: cheap and available in many different shapes and forms, it provides carbohydrates, some protein, "and it lasts forever," she says. There is an increasing awareness of the importance of carbohydrates. Current American guidelines suggest that these should supply 50–60 percent of the daily caloric intake.

Since weight-loss programs often come down hard on carbohydrates, we need to remember that it is *bread* that is the universal "staff of life."

Fiber can be added not only through whole-grain breads and cereals but also through what Dr. Swinamer describes as "free vegetables" — that is, vegetables which supply minerals, vitamins, and fiber, but almost no calories. In her list of such free vegetables, she includes mushrooms, celery, lettuce, cucumbers, and bean sprouts.

"People should keep these 'free' vegetables in mind when they are thinking of snacks for their children," Dr. Swinamer says. "And popcorn! Just think how inexpensive it is if you pop it yourself — and it fills without adding a whole lot of calories."

Dr. Swinamer believes in "value-added" meals — adding the value to inexpensive food by home cooking rather than eating preprocessed and packaged food. She herself loves to cook homemade soups like beef barley and vegetable and serve them with homemade biscuits. "Homemade food is much cheaper than processed," she says, "and almost all processed or prepackaged food is higher in fat, higher in salt, and lower in nutrition than the food you prepare yourself."

Like many nutritionists, Dr. Swinamer has a healthy scepticism about food fads that add to the cost of basic nutrition. The idea that "organically grown" food is somehow superior she dismisses as a "trendy popular myth." She would concur with the statement, "There is no scientific basis for claiming that organic foods are more nutritious than conventional foods. Food grown by chemical processes do not necessarily differ in taste, appearance, or nutrient content from those that are grown organically."[2] As a food producer, my husband is troubled by the way in which the media can swing public opinion on matters like "organically grown food." All food grows organically; there is no other way for it to grow. The nutrients that are transformed into food by a plant are the same, whether supplied by chemical or animal by-product fertilizer. The use of chemical fertilizers has brought about a consistent, low-priced supply of nutritious food. But today, nutritionally anxious young people may spend much more than is necessary for good food.

I asked Dr. Swinamer about some other "food anxieties" which may affect food habits, especially for nutritionally conscious people. Do we need vitamin supplements? Not usually, she thinks, provided we are eating a varied diet with a daily intake of fruit and vegetables. "But I don't think there is anything wrong with taking a one-a-day supplement," she says. "I wouldn't spend money on anything special, though — just a generic supplement. There is no evidence that we need such supplementation, but many people feel it's better to be on the safe side, and I see no problem with that."

And what about concerns that food from organs like liver are dangerous as sources of cholesterol? Dr. Swinamer thinks that liver is fine — and still an important source of iron. "If you keep your diet low-fat overall, you don't have to be unduly concerned about cholesterol," she says. And she dismisses worries about eggs as a source of cholesterol too. "Eggs are fine as long as the overall diet is low in fat. They are a good, cheap source of protein."

Dr. Swinamer sums up her healthy, informed, and balanced nutritional stance by saying, "Keep the fat down, and eat what you want!"

The 1990 Dietary Guidelines for Americans include the following:
1. Eat a variety of foods.
2. Maintain a healthy weight.
3. Choose a diet low in fat, saturated fat, and cholesterol.
4. Choose a diet with plenty of vegetables, fruits, and grain products.
5. Use sugars only in moderation.
6. Use salt and sodium only in moderation.
7. If you drink alcoholic beverages, do so in moderation.[3]

Shopping Tips

If you start from a position of basic understanding concerning the basic components of a balanced and nutritious diet, you can begin to plan shopping a little better. Especially on a limited budget, shopping is a task that demands real commitment and ability. Here are a few angles I learned in the lean years that might make your grocery cart a little easier to push around.

1. *Shop from a list.* This will help you avoid impulse buying, something which is promoted in every aisle of today's stores. Remember, your grocery store manager takes courses in how to tempt you to buy more than you need. You have to be prepared to outwit the most sophisticated psychological techniques as well as your own appetite if you are to keep your food basket uncluttered. Your shopping list can be made up in the following two ways, both of which I have used:

• *Draw up your list after planning your menus for the week.* This is a great idea for new homemakers, or for old ones who want to get out of food ruts. Planning this way will take you about an hour a week, after you have prepared a card index of menus with recipes to match. By following the basic food rules in setting up your menu cards, you can plan meals that are interesting and varied and nutritional. Then, looking up the recipes, you can list for purchase just those ingredients you will need for one week's meals. This is thrifty, and possibly the best way to teach yourself how to plan a balanced diet for your family.

• *Keep a running list of basic food supplies.* This should be fastened inside a cupboard door or somewhere else handy, with every member of the family jotting down items which need to be replenished as they run low. While I used the method outlined above for the first few years of marriage, this is the method we haved used for years in compiling our shopping lists. That's why my list used to show such items as "Toylet Payper," added by a seven-year-old making her contribution to keeping up basic supplies.

2. *Shop no more than once a week.* This may not be practical if you walk to your store and carry home your groceries, though there are small push-or-pull carts (and I don't mean the

ones that are supposed to be left at the store!) that you can get to bring home two or three bags. But if you drive to do your shopping, then once a week is the best way to shop. It has been my unfailing experience that every time I run into a grocery store for "some little thing" I neglected getting during my main shopping trip, I find myself picking up several other "little things," and food costs begin to escalate.

3. *Leave the children at home if you can.* Small children are precious and interesting, without a doubt. But in the aisles of a grocery store, they are just an added complication. Falling from grocery carts is now one of the most frequent causes of early childhood injury — so there, now you can leave them out of your grocery shopping trips for the sake of their health, instead of just your own.

It seems like a good division of labor for one member of the family to become the food-buying specialist. Whoever takes on that task should probably do the shopping alone if at all possible, without the interrupting assistance of little children. No matter how earnestly you may wish to take children's wishes into account, the time for children to express their food preferences is scarcely at the time you are trying to make price comparisons and keep the grocery cart off another shopper's heels.

By the time children are ten or so, they could be involved in helping with the shopping, and really taught how to shop — but earlier than that, they will add to both the cost and stress of a shopping trip. And when you are shopping on a very limited budget, there is plenty of stress built into family shopping without any additional pressure.

4. *Cut down on the number of canned and "almost ready" foods.* Most things are cheaper the further they are from being table-ready. And, as we have already discussed, the less packaged the food is, the lower its cost and the higher its nutritional value is likely to be. Peeling your own potatoes, soaking and baking your own beans, making your own soups, and buying pastas in bulk, instead of in ready-to-heat forms, are just some of the ways you can trim costs. The less you use your can

opener, the better. And, as a side benefit, the garbage gets easier to handle too.

5. *Skip the party foods aisle.* Tiny crackers, squeezable and disposable cheese packages, and other tidbit foods, many with built-in waste that still makes me wince, are often low in nutrition and high in cost. Even for party times, you might want to consider less expensive alternatives — such as your own hot-from-the-oven baking. Your guests are likely to be delighted with something plain and old-fashioned. I still remember one of the most memorable evening lunches ever served to me. It was served to us by Aunt Violet, an aunt of Cam's whom I met only the one time when, as newlyweds, we found ourselves in her town and dropped in for a visit. Caught with unexpected company, she served us tea accompanied by homemade bread and her own peach jam — all served with simple elegance and, best of all, without apology. Remembering that lunch helped me go on offering hospitality even when I could not afford expensive "fixings."

6. *Take it easy on the drinks.* Carbonated drinks, loaded with fizz and sugar and dye, may be popular with young people, but they do not make good nutritional sense. We found that we could save pop for special occasions — and then, most often, stretch it by adding it to fruit juice rather than serving it by itself. Powdered "fruit" drinks too strike me as an expensive way to buy dyed sugar. I still prefer to buy real fruit juice (usually frozen) and skim milk.

When our budget was at its tightest, we were blessed with having a cow to milk — not too feasible a solution for most of you, I imagine. But before we started milking for our family's needs, I mixed whole milk and reconstituted powdered skim milk in equal portions to reduce the cost of milk for four thirsty children. I found that mix — especially if I remembered to mix it up the night before and chill it well — stretched the milk budget without failing the taste test.

7. *Cut down on your use of paper or disposable plastic.* By making your own wipe-up rags from old clothes (soft T-shirts worn very thin are ideal), you can use, wash, and reuse instead

of buying disposable wipe-up cloths and towels. You can encourage your children to keep their tissues in their pockets for a second or third blow. Of course, this thrifty system often means that the tissues will go through the washing machine too! When it comes to paper products, what makes good economic sense makes good ecological sense, too. Just think, along with the dollars, of the trees your family can save.

8. *Buy less sugar and few presweetened products.* The rise in sugar consumption is a phenomenon of our affluence as a society. "Here is an example of how rising affluence over the years changes our kitchen habits," writes Doris Janzen Longacre. "My grandmother iced cakes only for birthdays. My mother iced most of her cakes, but thinly and only between the layers and on top — not on the sides. Until recently I stirred up an ample bowlful of frosting that covered everything and left plenty of finger-lickin's."[4]

Your family may be able to learn, as ours did, to get along with very much less sugar than we had at one time used. Remembering that natural sugars contained in fresh fruits and vegetables are better for us than processed sugar, we got used to meals without desserts apart from seasonal fruit, and that helped us trim not only our grocery budget but also our weight.

9. *Grow a garden.* Clearly, growing a garden is not an option for every family, though even apartment-dwellers might be able to find ways to grow at least salad vegetables in window-box or patio gardens. Because we lived on a farm where sometimes it seemed that the only thing we did have was space, we found growing a garden to be a great project for the whole family, with the homegrown vegetables providing a bonus in both nutrition and flavor. The children used to work with me in the garden. On hot days, we would set out a goal — perhaps, "Let's each hoe two rows" or "Let's get the peas picked," with the promise of a cool-down swim and picnic when the job was done. Unlike many of my neighbors, I never did get to be much of a canner or pickler or jam-maker, and I must be quite honest, I am still less than a rapturous gardener. But we did

work together as a family to put away each year all that we would need by way of frozen and root vegetables.

10. *In the midst of the pressure, grow a grateful heart.* It is easy to get focused on finances and forget how wonderfully we are provided for. And again, I suppose it was in the times when we no longer took daily and weekly provision for granted that we learned real gratitude. I can remember the cashier at our local co-op store wincing as she rang up the bill for my weekly shopping—which, by the time our kids were in their teens and we had a couple of hired people working in the summer, looked more like an order for a summer camp. "This is going to hurt," she said. Maybe because I have known times when I couldn't stock up, couldn't buy beyond the immediate needs, I could only protest, "Goodness, no. It doesn't hurt. I'm glad to have a family and hired people to feed and to live in a country where I can feed them."

In this hungry world of ours, where for many there is a daily struggle just to survive, we are the fortunate ones. Even when most pressed, most of us have only the problem of making wise choices.

Food, then, is first a matter of the head, as we study the facts of sound nutrition. And then it is a matter of the heart, as we share food lovingly with our families and with others. Sharing a meal is still the most open method of hospitality, the one which invites the outsider most deeply into the heart of your family life. Finally, food becomes a spiritual matter as we truly worship our Creator and Provider before each meal, not just in a mumbled grace, but in truly felt and clearly expressed gratitude.

Clothing

"If we have food and clothing, we will be content with that," writes Paul to the young pastor, Timothy (1 Tim. 6:8). And, as we meet our own needs and those of our family, we will have to group clothing with food as a "basic need." In *Fig-Leafing through History,* authors Christie Harris and Moira Johnston attack the notion that clothing is basically either for ornamentation or for seduction. Examining the history of costume, they conclude that clothing represents a very basic human need: the need to be covered.[5]

We need to be covered to define the line between our private and our public selves; to insulate our unfurred bodies from heat and cold; and to create a statement about our sense of self and self-worth. From the Genesis account of the Fall of our first parents in the Garden of Eden, we know that there is some link between clothing and our sense of sin, some way in which the transparency of relationships before the Fall is no longer available to us. But beyond that, we simply know that by modesty we transcend shame; that clothing, as it did in the Garden when God supplied Adam and Eve with animal skins to cover and warm them, continues to exemplify God's grace in dealing with us. And our care in dress demonstrates our appreciation for the bodies God has given us. How we look does affect the way we feel about ourselves—and the way in which others respond to us. Especially when we are in times of financial restraint, we need to find ways to celebrate ourselves in attractive clothing without overspending or becoming obsessed with the latest fashions.

Clothing our young people these days poses conundrums. While the things that frugal people have worn for years have become highly stylish, the young people I teach at the university are more likely than the working poor to wear ragged (and unpatched) jeans. There are always subtleties of brand name and styling to remind that these "looped and windowed" clothes are worn as a matter of choice and not of necessity.

In the matter of dress as well as the matter of food, we learned how faithfully God provides. Here—from my clothes closet to yours—are a few of the things we learned about clothing a growing family while having to keep up to date ourselves for lives which included political and professional involvement as well as platform speaking and television appearances—often on a shoestring budget.

1. *Sewing and mending.* In the '90s, torn and unpatched clothes have become trendy among teenagers—but most of us

are still glad to know how to patch and mend creatively. Tightening buttons as soon as a garment is purchased can sometimes save the frustration and expense of replacing a whole set of buttons. Patching worn children's clothes with bright fabric can extend the life of the garment and renew its style.

Even though I would rather write a book than thread a needle, I patched, mended, and sewed clothes for the children until they went to school. In fact, I became quite creative in the ways I mended whole boxes full of hand-me-downs from older cousins to keep the kids in renewed play clothes at little cost. When the sewing machine I had bought before I was married could no longer stand up to mending denim jeans and coveralls, I used one of my first writing checks to replace it. And I helped all my children learn how to use the sewing machine for projects of their own. Despite being among the least gifted seamstresses in the world, I still claim the credit for having taught our daughter Camille, now a doctor preparing to become a surgeon, how to take her first stitches.

For many years, my wardrobe was a handmade gift to me by an older woman in the community who took me into her heart when I arrived as a new bride about the same time her own children were leaving home. With a keen love for fabric and a strong sense of style, Elsie sewed for me (as well as for her daughters and daughter-in-law, all close to me in age and size), providing me with distinctive custom-made clothes I could never have afforded otherwise. She crowned the many years of loving ministry-by-needle by making wedding gowns for both of our daughters, each gown created with loving attention to detail and fitted to perfection by "Aunt Elsie."

For families where both spouses work outside of the home, the time that home-sewing takes would have to be evaluated against other claims. However, a sewing machine in the home means that sewing tasks as small as routine hemming or mending and as large as making new drapes can be done at a much lower cost than if they were custom done. (And, by the way, if you get joy out of sewing, doing these same tasks for others who do not have the time or equipment may be a source of income you can earn right at home.) For many stay-at-homers, sewing provides a double joy—the pleasures of frugality and of creativity. For some, it may also be a source of income or a mode of ministry.

2. *Recycling.* Buying good quality clothes at consignment or other types of resale stores no longer has any stigma attached. In fact, it is considered very smart to know how to find and wear a bargain. An acquaintance of mine who dresses like the model she once was, boasts that she has never yet spent more than fifty dollars on any one item of clothing—yet she always looks like a million. Her tip is that to spend a few dollars on a current fashion magazine (cheaper yet to read them at the public library) may save you several hundred in clothing purchases. Once you know the "look" you want, you can shop frugally at next-to-new stores.

When it comes to dressing children, I suggest you get in the slipstream just behind a family with children a year or two older than yours! Everyone needs to have someplace to send all those still-good clothes that are not worn out. It might as well be your house. I gladly received hand-me-downs, and made a newly arrived box a matter of celebration with the children. We would go through what was passed on to us with curiosity and delight (yes, and quite irreverent try-ons) and then choose what to keep and what to package up and pass on to the Salvation Army.

Pleasure at being able to share clothes was an old one for me. My mother had modeled the "gratitude attitude"; my sisters and I passed our clothes down to each other and later, when we were all much the same size, shared clothes to multiply our wardrobes. So I was stunned and very offended when one day I offered some outgrown clothes of our children's to a young mother. Though she had just been complaining about the high cost of kids' clothes, she drew herself up and replied scornfully, "We're not *that* hard up."

"Well," I said (and not as tranquilly as it looks in print), "I guess we have always been that hard up." I have never thought that recycling good clothes was evidence of anything but good sense, glad sharing, and God's provision.

3. *Shopping and selection.* Shopping at end-of-season sales still strikes me as one of the best ways to buy new clothes at reasonable prices. The winter clothing needed in the northern states and in Canada is expensive, but much less so if you can watch for the late winter clearance sales and outfit your family a year ahead.

As children grow up, they need to have a greater voice in their clothing choices. After all, they are the ones who have to wear those clothes among their schoolmates. Clothing is a powerful element in establishing self-esteem, especially among today's status-conscious young.

I needed to be reminded of that by my own teenagers. I recall driving to town for shopping with them one day. In the backseat, I could hear discussion about what brand was "in" and what was "out." In a voice of maternal authority, I pronounced, "The brand name just doesn't matter."

"Oh," said my son's voice from behind me, "but it does, Mom, it does."

And he was, of course, right. In the culture in which the kids lived, brand names were part of the silent language of the hallways. The only way I could solve the tension between my sense of "value" and theirs was to assign to each of them a clothing allowance and let them make their own choices. If buying one pair of jeans "shot the wad," they would have to wait for other items on their lists. They learned to save for big-ticket items and to make choices, and, as a result, we didn't have so many arguments to deal with.

* * *

"See how the lilies grow," Jesus said (Matt. 6:28). From the field flowers, we can learn not only of God's good provision, but the joy of individuality and variety, the fun of color and texture. Clothing, carefully chosen and tastefully worn, need not be an endless hassle and should not be a source of worry. Rather, as a carefully thought-through and well-planned part of life, clothing becomes a joyful affirmation of our personal dignity and worth, and a source of praise to God, the giver of all good gifts.

Ten Ways to Save Money Now

1. Examine credit card spending. Studies indicate that the convenience of a credit card results in a 30 percent increase in spending.

2. Stay out of shopping malls. The average time spent per visit to a shopping mall is 69 minutes. Only 52 percent of shoppers surveyed spend less than one hour when shopping. A lot of damage can be done in one hour with your credit card.

3. For a good return on investment, pay your credit card debt. The interest charges you save in paying off your credit card debt are much higher than the interest you would receive if you had an investment of equal value at a bank.

4. Begin saving tax dollars. Read the tax credits and deductions listed in the booklet with your income tax return. Retirement fund contributions and charitable donations are two examples of how you can plan for retirement and reduce taxes. Consider making a contribution to your retirement fund and giving the refund to charity.

5. Compare auto insurance rates. Rates can vary substantially from one agency to another, and the quality of coverage may be the same. The benefits from researching rates and coverage can add up real savings!

6. Examine your grocery shopping bill. Begin using coupons and purchasing sale items only. You will watch your food expenditures drop by 15 percent.

7. If you eat lunch in restaurants during the week, limit this to one day per week, and not payday (you will spend too much). You will save nearly $30 per week, and this may total $1,500 in a year!

8. Decide to save a portion of your income each week. Even $5 per week will give you over $250 extra at year end.

9. If you are traveling on the same route as family members or coworkers, consider carpooling. Sharing expenses with only one other person will reduce transportation costs by 50 percent, provide companionship for the ride, and help our environment!

10. Prepare a gift list. Plan your gift ideas, and purchase them in advance when gift items are on sale. Better still, make a gift; it will be special and have far more value to the recipient.

Remember, last-minute shopping always costs more, sometimes up to 40 percent!

— Used by permission from "His Ways & Our Means," January 1994, © Inter-Varsity Christian Fellowship of Canada.

Chapter Eight

Basic Needs III:
Housing and Wheels

Wheels

Like many families, we found the problem of providing adequate housing for our family to be a difficult one. While food and clothing are the bare minimum basics when it comes to needs, nobody disputes that housing is an essential too. Bewildered by ever-rising costs of home construction and struggling with straightening out real housing values — space for a family, sufficient individual privacy, warmth for our long, cold winters — from those confusing transferred values — status, snobbery, "pride of life," we spent several winters in cramped rented accommodations as we thought and prayed and waited.

Part of the North American way of life until the last two or three decades has been not only a place to call home but a place to call your own. Even a Willy Loman, the loser salesman in Arthur Miller's *Death of a Salesman,* is able to buy a little house and put himself into fixing it up. Today, the high costs of land and housing have pushed this possibility of home ownership well out of the reach of many people, or pushed young married people into the necessity of earning two incomes in order to meet heavy payments on long-term mortgages.

We have to face the fact that the inaccessibility of affordable family dwellings reflects not only the high cost of housing, but also the high cost of furnishings. Television has piped the big dream into our living rooms for so many hours that we really begin to think of "home" in terms of the sets for television dramas. We have to struggle to remember that the shows have been brought to us, hour after hour, by the producers of goods who want us to want and consume things and who encourage us to develop extravagant tastes so that we will buy, buy, and go on buying.

I learned quite a bit by living in the tiny house the Lord provided for us as a "shelter in the time of storm." Our family of six lived in about 800 square feet of space (not counting a damp basement, where there was space for my washer and drier). There were three small bedrooms, two of them upstairs under the eaves, with the bats twittering in the attic on the other side of the thin walls and occasionally escaping into the house. We turned the downstairs bedroom into an office and finally made the living room double as a bedroom by means of a convertible sofa. We felt cramped, all right. If one of the kids brought a balloon home from a party, I felt as though someone was going to have to leave to make room for it. And then there was the time when all the kids and Cam got mumps together!

Certainly, compared with the houses people were building around us, our housing was inadequate, and yet we had to stop once in awhile to remember that a generation earlier, a family of four grew to adulthood in this very house. A family of six plus a hired girl. What had changed? Were children bigger than they had been a generation ago? Or were our housing concepts just bigger?

We had to admit, as we thought about it, that our need for large houses reflects our growing accumulation of things far more than a real need for more space for people. It is particularly ironic that as houses get bigger, families get smaller. Let's face it, more and more people are finding they just cannot afford both a big house and a big family. Because we had to do a lot of thinking about housing, we became aware of a range of resourceful solutions to the problem of adequate housing. Perhaps one of these will be the solution for you, as it was for us.

1. *Work to save a down payment and then buy a modest house.*

You can take a twenty-five or thirty-year mortgage, recognizing that housing always costs (usually about 24 percent of disposable income), but that real estate has customarily responded to inflation. This means that your home, if well maintained, is likely to increase in value over the years. Home ownership has been one of the "little person's" surest investments, supplying a basic need for the family as the property value increases.

2. *Buy an older, run-down house and have the joy of restoring it to life.* This, of course, depends on your having the skills for renovating, since that will represent the "sweat equity" you put into your house and recover when you sell it. Even more, it will depend upon the whole family having the patience to live in the mess of ongoing construction—something not everyone can stand. But if you have the skills and temperament for living in a half-finished project, it may work for you. We know a successful building contractor who started his business in just this way, moving into a run-down house, upgrading it and then reselling it. Then he moved into another and did the same, until he had the capital—and the experience—he needed for launching his own custom building business. Nor does this method of home ownership provide only inexpensive housing for the family. It also provides ongoing renewal for urban areas which might otherwise downgrade into slums. On the negative side, of course, are the social problems of "gentrification," by which renewed and renovated older homes in centrally located urban neighborhoods become trendy homes for the well-to-do young and are pushed up in price out of the reach of the poor. If you are considering this buy-up-grade-sell approach to gradually improving your housing, you might also have to consider whether you are comfortable with moving your family into the kind of neighborhood in which run-down houses tend to be found. What kind of schools are there? How safe are the streets? After weighing the pros and cons, you may decide that this is the right choice for you. And if you do, think about looking for a church just around the corner, and becoming part of the ministry in the area in which

you are living. That way you can become part of building something more permanent even than your home.

3. *Buy a house with an apartment in the basement or else-where.* Be sure before doing this to check zoning regulations to ascertain that you can legally rent it out. Or move into a duplex and rent the other half. You will have to give up some of your privacy and some of the elegance of a place all to yourself, but the extra revenue could well cover your mortgage payments, thus making it possible for you to purchase your own real estate.

4. *Consider the possibility of building your own place.* This is something which more and more young people are doing now. You can buy precut houses, or save even more by buying the dimensional lumber and building a home yourself. Be realistic in estimating your savings, remembering that you will still have to hire subcontractors to do the work in which you are not skilled. And don't forget that it will take time and grit to see a project like this through to completion. Some additional precautions are: Be sure to check carefully the housing regulations covering the area where you intend to build; remember that you will need help and perhaps a labor exchange with one or more friends. Outside of city limits (or even within some), you may be able to build a basement and finish enough to live in it, and then build your house over your head. Habitat for Humanity, the home-building program that ex-President Jimmy Carter has made so visible, may provide a way for you to build—or help someone else to build—a place to call home. (Habitat for Humanity International, Inc., 121 Habitat Street, Americus, GA 31709-3498.)

5. *Build, or have built, a small house with a design and on a lot which are suitable to future expansion.* This may be a way to save interest if you can pay for the first part of the house before going on with the next phase. Friends of ours have built a spacious family home in this way. Starting with a cozy two-bedroom bungalow when they were first married, they have expanded the house in two phases as the needs of their family have grown, imaginatively adapting a simple basic plan to meet

their family's special tastes and requirements.

6. *If you already own a home, consider all the possibilities for developing your present property.* A developed basement or attic or a built-on addition may be enough to make your house meet your family's needs, probably at far less expense than buying a new home at today's prices. When Barb and Jim found that their three-bedroom bungalow, bought ten years ago, was beginning to feel a bit snug, they began to look at new housing. When they calculated the cost of a move to a larger house, they found that they could much more economically develop the one they already had. A basement development project doubled the amount of their living space at far less cost than the same number of square feet would cost at today's prices. My cousin Rodger Woods is an architect who has found a way to make a small old brick house big enough for his family through the ingenious use of the existing space and the planning (and hand-building) of several additions: first, kitchen and dining areas, later, an expanded upstairs. There are many exciting ways to make your present home "do," providing that you own it and can get city council approval for proposed renovations.

7. *A more radical idea, but one that is increasingly interesting to young families, is to solve your housing problems away from a major city.* Consider moving out to the country and buying an old farmhouse to rebuild, or building your own new home on an acreage or in a small town. But don't let the lure of the land draw you into an ill-advised move. Consider carefully the job opportunities suitable to your skills within a reasonable driving radius. A necessity for this way of life is dependable vehicles, probably two, since a person left stranded ten miles from anywhere is sure to feel insecure. So include the cost of extra transportation in your figuring. And be sure you get someone experienced in home building to assess the soundness and give you an estimate of the cost of fixing up that romantic old house you fall in love with before you start in on something quite unrealistic.

The advantages of this approach to housing are becoming

apparent to more and more young people who like the idea of raising their children away from the "thickening centre."[1] We are seeing farmhouses that have stood empty for years being bought and lived in. Five-acre plots can still be purchased in more remote rural areas for a fraction of the cost of an average city lot. I am not talking about moving to the plush acreage suburbs of a large city which are customarily inhabited by doctors, lawyers, and chiropractors. Rather, I am referring to getting far out into the country, a hundred miles or more from major cities. Only then is there any real economy in this concept. And I am *not* talking about "going farming" as a way to solve the housing dilemma. Farming is a big business and a risky one. Trying to live off the land is to reduce living to a subsistence, virtually no-cash level, which is very difficult for inexperienced or even experienced people. What I am talking about is practicing your trade or profession in a small town or city within a reasonable driving radius (probably 50 miles or so) and enjoying the quiet of country or small-town living. You can live for less in the country because you can grow your own garden, keep a cow, and raise chickens – and children – on a place of your own. You need fewer "good" clothes, but transportation is expensive and continuous. Utilities characteristically cost a great deal more than in the city, but you have to develop and maintain your own water and sewage system outside of a town or city. So everything does not come up roses. However, it is an option worth considering – carefully.

8. *A low-cost answer to housing is mobile or prefab homes.* Mobile homes sometimes do not have the status, the eye appeal, or the prestige of other homes. And, unfortunately, many of the subdivisions in urban areas for mobile homes are unattractive and ridiculously crowded. However, more and more municipalities are beginning to zone proper-sized lots for mobile homes, recognizing that mobile homes do not represent transience as much as lower-cost housing, deserving of dignity as a practical solution to the pressing problem of housing for young families. One thing that must be weighed against the initial price advantage is that mobile homes have customarily

depreciated in value, while properly maintained fixed dwellings customarily appreciate. Quality of insulation and wiring needs to be carefully checked, since the fire hazard of mobile homes, with the large amount of flammable glue used in their construction, must be taken into consideration.

9. *Obviously, apartment or semidetached dwellings will increasingly be the normal housing for most newly married urban couples and for many families as well.* Since there is a wide range of differences as well as costs in today's apartments and condominiums, this may be the kind of housing which you prefer, or it may be what you can afford. Whatever the case, your apartment home can be "a light shining in a dark place" (2 Peter 1:19), your family a Christian witness in the apartment or condominium complex in which you live. The very proximity to other people, which often affords many problems, can also offer limitless opportunities to befriend, to witness, to show the love and life of Christ. Many choose this type of housing, knowing that home ownership involves a multitude of other concerns and costs: lawns to be mowed, storm windows put up and taken down again, and an endless round of maintenance. When I have watched apartment dwellers place their key cards in the automatic door opener of their underground garage, I have mused about the simple life. All the folklore to the contrary, the simple life may well be apartment living.

Which of these was our solution?

Well, we had property in the country, so it made sense to build there. A year or two after our business failed, we had our financial affairs in order again and approached the credit manager of our credit union. Would it be possible for us to get a mortgage for a very modest home? We had priced out mobile homes and had some figures for him. We had sat there so often, it seemed: Going over figures, explaining our situation and our plan for repayment of debt, making payments. We waited anxiously while he looked at our proposal and then across his desk at us. In my mind I rehearsed what I thought we would hear: It would, I thought, sound something like, "We certainly understand your need for a home, but your present circumstances would not allow for any further extension of credit. . . ." Or, perhaps, "Why don't you come back and see us in a year or two?"

Instead, the credit manager stubbed out his cigarette and cleared his throat and said, "You folks don't really want a mobile home, do you? Why don't you go get some prices on a house and bring them in to me."

We did. With his encouragement, we shopped for a modest plan that we could modify to meet our needs, determined not to borrow one more dollar than we needed to supply our family with a comfortable home. And then we had the house built. By building into a hill so that the front of the basement was ground level and full of light, and by developing both upper and lower levels fully, we had ample space under a small roof, doubling our 1,250 square feet in living space. What a joy to have a generous entryway with a wash-up bathroom at the back door, a laundry room, an office, small but adequate bedrooms for each of the children, a separate playroom, and a "great room," a large open living-dining-kitchen area. We even have a tiny *en suite* bathroom off our compact "master bedroom." This was not the glossy show-home of the "country homes" magazines, but a comfortable, affordable home suited to our needs as a family. We had lots of windows to let in light from all directions, lots of walls to gradually fill in with bookshelves, and a special wall in the open living-dining-kitchen area where, years later, we would install a beautiful cast iron wood-burning stove on a raised hearth, set against a blue-gray stone facing.

When we moved into our new home, our children were in elementary school; through the rest of their growing-up years, the home fit our family like a glove — sometimes a very snug glove. True enough, one of the kids had to give up a bedroom when company came; for several years a spare cot in the laundry room was where one of them slept during the summers we had live-in hired help for our farm. Later, we were able to move a separate small summer house onto our farmstead, for "extras."

"Today's home buyer wants space that can be adjusted to meet new needs over time. . . . Secondary bedrooms [are] proportionally bigger. And the addition of private bathrooms makes them better suited for use down the road by adult children or older parents who return to the home,"[2] declared a recent newspaper article.

Well in advance of such housing trends being announced, we built our fully finished ground-level basement floor so that it could serve as a separate suite of rooms, thinking that perhaps one day one of our parents might need a sunny sitting room, bedroom, and bathroom.

Our children grew up and we moved on, but the house again shelters a young family—now it is our son's family that shelters there, and we have down-sized to a snug, light-filled city apartment, just big enough for the two of us.

Whatever the solution to meeting the housing needs of your family, the real joys of any home are not in the size or shape of the physical plant, but in the spirit of love and contentment that prevails within the walls. As you learn contentment in the situation in which you find yourself, you can trust God to guide you in making the necessary adjustments to make housing adequate for your needs.

Wheels

The ever-present cost pressure of owning and then of operating a family vehicle or two involves major decision-making. When friends of ours decided they had to supplement their family station wagon with a second car, they found an old Ford with a lot of its gray paint chipped off. It was a kind of sad-looking car that their teen sons immediately dubbed "Dog Face." One of the boys' pals looked at the car and hooted, "What's that thing supposed to be?"

"That," said my friend, with the immense dignity she saves for such moments, "is a one-payment car."

They had decided on one of the three options that seem to make good economic sense when it comes to providing dependable transportation at a reasonable cost. Here are the low-cost options as I see them. One may be right for you.

1. *Buy a low-cost used car and drive it until it begins to need major repairs.* When a car begins to burn oil, major motor problems are probably just around the corner. If you suspect problems with either the engine or the transmission, you should probably take the car to a nondealer mechanic and ask for an assessment. Before authorizing any work, you can then decide if the cost of fixing the car is more than the car is worth to you and if so, sell it and start again.

While you can compromise on cosmetics (a car does not have to be pretty), you will want to be uncompromising on safety: tires, brakes, and steering. And for safety's sake, you need to do your trouble-shooting before the car lets you down. Nonetheless, if you need to drive an old car, you might want to consider membership in a motorist association that provides emergency help and towing if necessary. Your car insurance, however, likely will reimburse you for towing.

2. *Buy a premium used car.* This is different from buying a "junker" and driving it until it drops. Buying a premium used car means buying a car of which you know the history, or one which is in excellent condition, and maintaining it for all the extra miles that are in it after its initial depreciation has brought the price down.

After we had watched neighbors buy the two- or three-year-old cars we had traded for newer models, and drive them for another five or six years, we began to take this thrifty route too. Cam tells me that in shopping for a used car, he looks for any indication (beyond the mileage on the odometer) that tells how much, and how hard, the car has been driven. "I look for wear on the brake pedal," he says, since that is one indicator of use that cannot be easily touched up. "And look for any indications of touch-up activity: little spray-over jobs covering rust spots, for instance. I take a close look at the upholstery to see if there are little nicks or tears that, despite a cleanup, would be signs of hard or careless use. And if the car were full of the smell of pine trees, I'd try to figure out what the pine trees were trying to cover.

"I'd avoid any car that looks like it has seen country roads — little gravel chips in the paint, or bent parts underneath. And I'd also avoid anything that had what the kids call 'wide skins' or tires with bold white lettering — which would suggest it has been driven by a teenager.

"I would, of course, pull the dipstick. Usually that's all looked after in preparing a car for sale, of course, but just in case — I'd take a look at the oil. If it were at all dirty, I wouldn't buy. And when I took the car for a test drive, I would check it for overall tightness — in the steering, the drive train, the body.

"If I can get a chance to meet the previous owner, all the better," Cam stresses. "I can study the kind of person who owned the car before — the house and yard, the clothing and attitude. I'm looking for any indication of owner attitude toward the vehicle I am considering buying — and the more persnickety and fussy that person appears to be, the better for me. Of course, I'll ask the reasons for selling the car — and evaluate what the owner tells me."

Sometimes Cam has bought cars directly from their previous owners; sometimes he has bought through a dealer. When we're ready to replace our current car, he lets a salesperson or two know what he is looking for — placing a tentative order and hoping to hear of a good quality car that has come in on trade. And Cam takes a look at a current *Consumer Guide* rating. "A low-mileage lemon may look like a good deal but cost you a lot in the long run," he points out. "I'm more interested in a highly rated car, even if it has been driven a bit longer."

What about the car you are driving right now? "Sell it privately or give it to one of your kids or the mechanic down the street — you'll probably do just as well as trying to trade it in on another used car," Cam says. He points out that the car price jumps approximately 15 percent the minute that a trade-in is involved. Cam suggests that if you really want to unload your current car in the deal, begin the discussion on a no-trade basis so that a price can be established. Then you can ask what the price would look like if you offered your trade-in, and you'll know exactly the difference, exactly what your old used car is deemed to be worth.

The trend in North America toward people keeping their cars longer works against the "premium used car" route to affordable transportation, since it means fewer next-to-new cars on the market and at higher prices than a few years ago. It is still worth taking a look. We have been able to enjoy the comfort and low-cost miles of excellent cars which, had we bought them new, would have cost us a lot more.

3. *Buy a new car and drive it until it reaches the end of its tether.* Perhaps that will be eight or ten years, depending on the number of miles you drive per year. This plan requires that you maintain the car carefully so that it lasts and lasts and lasts. The high depreciation of the first year or two are spread out over as many as ten years, and thus a car bought new can be quite economical.

Of course, there are still many people who can afford to buy new cars every year or two, but others either cannot afford this style or are wondering if there are not more useful ways of spending their money. More and more, people are availing themselves of short courses in mechanical know-how, borrowing or renting garage space, and doing minor and even major repairs on their own vehicles.

A major factor in any new- or used-car decision is gas-mileage economy. For the sake of both economy and the environment, many of us are looking for ways to find our groceries — and probably our church fellowship — within walking distance of our homes, instead of trekking across our cities in endlessly crisscrossing patterns. Who knows? The cost of fuel may even have the effect of keeping some families home together in the evenings, giving them a chance to get to know each other again. Many of us are learning to leave the car in the garage whenever we can, to keep lists so that we make a minimum number of trips to stores, and to walk or bike instead of driving. These "new" concepts of how to get around represent not only savings in expense but also improvement in general physical condition. Walking, jogging, and biking can give us the warm, happy, and slightly choking sensation that we are merely using up pollution instead of creating it.

*   *   *

A place to call home, a means by which to get away from and back to it again, plus our food and clothing constitute basic physical needs. For these we can, in faith, claim God's supply, while at the same time learning to be judicious in our choices.

Chapter Nine

The Other Needs

The young pastor's wife came home from the seminar, crushed and bewildered. "I guess I just don't have enough faith," she said.

"Enough faith for what?" I wondered aloud.

"Well," she explained, "the speaker was telling us how to budget our time and money. But she was so breezy about economic matters. She told us, 'I just believe God wants to give you all good things. Why, He just loves to give you the desires of your heart. Right now, I'm asking the Lord for a South Pacific cruise. And, you know, it's beginning to look as though one is shaping up for us.' " My friend came away from the seminar sick at heart. "A lot of us just don't live at that level. Is it lack of faith? The desire of my heart is to feed and clothe the kids on my husband's salary, never mind the South Pacific cruise!"

The young wife was quite right; most of us do not live at a level where we have the liberty to think of doing some of the things which seem to come so naturally to others. For such a high standard of living to be held out as a norm, achievable by any who dare to exercise faith, is a travesty of Christian values.

A.W. Tozer writes scathingly, "So many professing Christians just want to get things from God. Anyone can write a book now that will sell — just give it a title like *Seventeen Ways to Get Things from God!* ... Many people seem to be interested in knowing God for what they can get out of Him."[1] In another article, entitled "That Utilitarian Christ," Tozer warns against viewing the Lord Jesus Christ as "a kind of Aladdin's lamp to do minor miracles in behalf of anyone who summons Him," and goes on to say:

> The whole purpose of God in redemption is to make us holy and to restore us to the image of God. . . . He disengages us from earthly ambitions and draws us away from the cheap and unworthy prizes that worldly men set their hearts upon.[2]

From the Reformation acceptance of the intrinsic worth of secular vocations, and the necessity for hard work within those callings, we have moved so far toward complete secularization of our lives that we need to carefully examine everything we read or hear to see if it sounds at all like the lowly Jesus, who had no place to call home, no coin with which to pay His taxes, no wealth except that of the Spirit. And before we lightly quote verses of Scripture as magic passkeys to material blessings, we need to ask seriously about God's purposes in our lives. We must always be aware and afraid of treating God as some kind of heavenly vending machine which will spew out endless material things for our enjoyment simply because we have "faith" and live uprightly.

"God is Spirit: and His worshipers must worship in spirit and in truth" (John 4:24). He is concerned about our material needs insofar as they constitute real needs; Jesus taught us that in the Sermon on the Mount. If, in His bounty, God should give us a measure of prosperity over and above our needs, that is a gift of His disposing, not of our demanding. And it is given to us in trust.

A few years ago, some friends of ours listened to a sermon on faith. The speaker told the story of two women, a mother and a daughter, who were in need of winter coats. The mother prayed (as a member of an older generation might), "Dear Lord, I need a winter coat. Just anything, as long as it is warm, will do." The daughter (a true member of the modern society) prayed, "I need a winter coat too, Lord. But, please, I would like it to be brand-new, size twelve, and green." Each woman got exactly what she had asked for, the preacher said. The gist of the sermon seemed to be: Ask for lots — the very best — and you will get it. Our friends took the sermon very seriously. They understood its message and acted on it. About to build a new house, they scrapped modest, budget-fitting plans they had been thinking about and built a much larger home that brought them to the brink of insolvency.

As economic pressures on the average family increase in the days ahead, we need to speak out against any kind of teaching which suggests that God exists to make us rich, that His special joy is in doling out things. Nothing could be farther from the spirit of the New Testament. There, the dangers of riches are solemnly warned against (for example, 1 Tim. 6:10). There, the norm is "be content with what you have" (Heb. 13:5). There, earthly goods are something to be held in trust; a person's earnings are to enable him to care for his own family and to share with others.

I am sure that many of God's children have known times when God has been pleased to give them the sudden surprise of some delightful material gift. But for the one who is intent on knowing God, that thing, however wonderful it may be, is nothing compared with the hand that gives it, the hand of the great unchangeable giver of all good gifts.

If we study carefully what Jesus said, we will understand that we have no need to be anxious about the supply of our basic needs. They are our right as sons and daughters, heirs in the family of God and will be supplied. But He gives no warrant anywhere for whining and pleading with God for more than our needs, and Paul in his emphasis on self-control echoes his Lord. We can make our requests known. That is our privilege. But to demand, to claim promises out of context, and to expect that righteous behavior should have some earthly tangible reward is pathetically to miss the point.

Charles H. Spurgeon, in commenting on the verse, "You

may ask Me for anything in My name, and I will do it" (John 14:14), makes this thought-provoking observation:

> I may not ask for anything to which I cannot put Christ's hand and seal. I dare not use my Lord's name to a selfish or willful petition. I may only use my Lord's name to a prayer which He would Himself pray if He were in my case. It is a high privilege to be authorized to ask in the name of Jesus as if Jesus Himself asked; but our love to Him will never allow us to set that name where He would not have set it.[3]

I remember one long-ago spring when I had to wait for what seemed an insufferably long time for my paycheck for a part-time job I had taken. I had gone to the university during the winter and had that familiar flat-broke feeling many students have after eight months of steady withdrawals and no deposits. Besides that, I had seen a suit—a beautiful pink suit—in a downtown store. It was lovely and well within the buying power of that check, if and when it would come. Every time I was downtown, I looked to see if the suit was still there. And every time the postman arrived, I looked for that check. Days passed. Still no check. One day, fighting the disappointment of yet another day without the paycheck, I was washing dishes in our basement apartment and arguing with the Lord about it all. "But," I complained, "I've earned that check. Couldn't you just remind someone to mail it to me?" And then a Scripture came so forcibly into my mind that I set down the glass I was washing and listened to it. "When you ask, you do not receive because you ask . . . so that you may spend what you get on your pleasures" (James 4:3).

There were tears in my eyes, but I responded, "OK, Lord. It's not a need. It's just a want." When at the last that check did arrive, I no longer "needed" the pink suit at all.

Over a good many years, even as a very slow learner, I have come to see that far more wonderful than God's giving us every whim we place before Him is the complete—if sometimes painful—job He can do of taking a want out of my heart and then filling the hole it leaves with joy and contentment.

Of course, over and above the basic needs, there are legitimate and recognized needs of the human spirit, mind, and body. With some creative use of available resources, many of these needs too can be met within limited budgets. And life can be full of "extras" without big price tags attached.

1. *The need for spiritual and intellectual stimulation and growth.* I remember listening to my hairdresser, Richard, chattering as he jerked my head and snipped my hair. "There are some people I know, like, they seem to need to go to every training session on the continent. We had a girl, like, in one of our shops, like, who spent every holiday and all of her money traveling from one hairdressing course to another. And, like, I don't think it has too much to do with learning. Just seems that some people, like, just need to go to all those deals to get sort of pepped up—to believe in themselves. But me, I'd just as soon spend my holidays, like, relaxing. I can learn all I need from the trade magazines. Like, guys who run those short courses have gotten very, very rich because of people who just need that kind of inspiration."

I listened with interest because what Richard was saying can be applied to the endless conferences and seminars that many Christians spend their time and money and holidays attending. There is no doubt that we all need fellowship. We all need encouragement. And we all need inspiration from time to time. I have spoken at lots of conferences (without, by the way, getting rich at it) and have letters on file to remind me that these times of getting together for instruction in the Word of God and for mutual encouragement do change lives.

If we have the money to travel for conferences and seminars, then it is a good way to promote personal growth. But if such programs are beyond the reach of our budgets, we need not despair. I have found that God is just as accessible from the square of linoleum that is my kitchen floor as He is from the loftiest mountaintop conference. In fact, when the children were all preschoolers at once, I found the only "retreat center" I could get to was the bathroom.

In the years when we were starting our farming business and our family, many of our just slightly younger friends were knapsacking across Europe, spending some time at L'Abri. Others of our more-established friends were going half-way around the world to attend conferences. I learned, in those years, to answer the question, "Where could I go?" in the words of the spiritual song: "Just to the Lord." Shut in with my family in a tiny farmhouse in Alberta, I found ways to go on growing.

I pored over catalogs of advanced learning programs and seminars in distant and exotic places, and then I settled down to read what the greatest writers have said and thought. I learned to grow mentally and spiritually right in my home. I made reading lists from course outlines and book reviews, and read systematically in whole periods of English literature. I read and reread the Bible often, searching the whole of the Bible for understanding a particular topic. So I was able to go on growing at minimal dollar cost.

I yearned for the day when I would be able to engage in more formal study—and rejoiced when that opportunity did come. But in the meanwhile, I did not sigh and resign myself to stagnation while such opportunities were out of reach, both geographically and financially.

The "need to know" can be satisfied, if you have the means, by formal study or by travel. Lacking those means, it can still be satisfied—or better, whetted—by making use of library facilities. Travel to distant places may be beyond the family budget, but good books, maps, and a globe can help you visit faraway places at little or no expense from the warmth of your own home. Cultivating correspondence with various friends across the world will bring exotic foreign stamps to your mailbox while enlarging the worldview of your whole family. Entertaining in your home will bring the world into your living room.

We recall one evening when, in the little kitchen of our farm home, missionaries from Ethiopia met an agricultural exchange trainee from England. Our guests from Africa began to talk with our boarder from England, and within five minutes they discovered that they had a mutual acquaintance: a young woman who was a daughter of the missionaries' coworkers was in nurses' training with the fiancée of our exchange trainee. For a few exciting moments we felt like we were at the crossroads of the world!

Maintaining our *oneness* with the members of the body of Christ brings news from around the world into our home in the form of letters and mission magazines. We reach back out to that world in giving, in prayer, and in letters. Over the years, through Christian fellowship and other connections, we have established a network of personal friends so that now we have friends in almost every free country on the globe. When and if we should be enabled to travel, there will be friends to greet us wherever we go. That's one of the great pleasures of functioning as part of "the family of God." Meanwhile, with young children, we found that the happiest vacations were spent close to home. Frequent short jaunts to the lake twenty miles from our home, sometimes expanded into overnight camping, were as much fun for our children when they were small as the longer trips we attempted.

Our kids still recall the minor epic journey we made, on a sudden impulse, one Saturday afternoon. We went to a town "down the line" from where we lived — about an hour's drive — and did all the things that people do on holidays: Took a room in a motel, ate Chinese food at a restaurant, and went out to see a Disney double feature. (Yes, they even remember what they saw: *The Legend of Lobo* and *Dumbo*. They cried in both of them.) It was a case of making a lot of memories by spending only a little money. For some reason, we all still remember the magic of that weekend. To our now-grown kids, it is as memorable as most of the longer holidays we took with them as they grew older.

2. *The need for aesthetic pleasure.* There is a very real need of the human mind and spirit to perceive and to create things of aesthetic beauty. The God who "hath made everything

beautiful in His time" (Ecc. 3:11) is the one who, in making us in His image, has planted within us the desire for beauty. It is no pagan wish. Neither is it one which requires wealth to satisfy. Aesthetic appreciation can be developed even if your budget precludes you from concerts and performances of the fine arts. Television brings some fine performances into your home, at little cost. You can enjoy the best of good music on your tape or CD player, purchasing an endless number of listenings for about the price of a good seat in a concert hall. Museums and art galleries are customarily free to visit. And, again, there are books.

But, of course, aesthetic appreciation should not just be reserved for formal expressions. A friend, home on furlough from an appointment in North Africa, strolled with me down our lovely lane. "After the endless brown of dried-out northern Africa, the green is so beautiful," she commented. She noted the shades of green against the blue, late afternoon sky. "You know, I have really come to appreciate the *ministry of nature.*" Learning to see, to really see, the beauty of the world around us requires nothing more than the use of the senses with which we come equipped. And whether we look at the patch of sky that is ours from a city window or at a sweeping vista on a country road, we can feed our hearts on beauty until praise is born.

The desire to create things of beauty has been exploited in a booming business in craft kits and do-it-yourself (almost) outfits. Crafts and hobbies are an enrichment of life, but some of them may be out of reach when the budget is tight. Remember, though, that the essence of crafts is "creativity." Thus, the more creative you are in seeing the resources available to you, the more satisfying you will find them. You could try hobby-swapping with friends. When the excitement of their rock tumbler has passed, your family may have exhausted the possibilities of candle-making equipment. So arrange an exchange. Again, the library is your pass to free and inexpensive crafts. Books abound to get you and your family started in developing an artistic or creative bent. If you cannot afford to oil paint, you can surely sketch with pencil or charcoal. And poetry has been written on all sorts of surfaces; you could even use the backs of envelopes for that, as Emily Dickenson did.

Creative expression in music requires some sort of instrument (the least expensive, of course, is the voice), some training, and a great deal of persistent practice. In the mid-'70s we visited in a country home that was still without running water or electric power. But an old upright Bell piano sat against one living room wall, with a propane lamp nearby and sheaves of music piled around. The woman, over eighty and bent with age, sat down and played. Her husband sang in a mellow — if somewhat quavery — tenor voice. He no longer plays his violin, he said, "But that grandson of mine, he can get a great tune out of that fiddle." Poor? Enriched by an afternoon of home-grown music, I thought not. Our little home was loud with music since the children all took piano lessons. In the days before our house was built, we were blessed with such a lack of space that the piano and television were in the same room. By the time three children had practiced after school, there was little time for television viewing. Cam and I would sit in the kitchen while in the living room Cammie picked out a tune on her guitar and on the porch Geoff blasted away on a second-hand trumpet. We wanted music to be part of the intangible riches our children would come to value, and having bought a secondhand piano as one of our earliest household purchases, gave music lessons priority over other "wants" even in our most stringent budgets. Three out of four of our children express appreciation for that — either enjoying musical performances or playing instruments themselves. A fourth still feels it was a waste of money and an encroachment on his life. Well, three out of four is not bad!

3. *The need to feel secure.* This is another need which is hard for people on tight budgets to meet. Security. Peace of mind. And these days, these are not easy to come by. Even when we put away payments in government pension plans, we find ourselves wondering if there is going to be money to meet com-

mitments as the demographic bulge called "The Baby Boom" reaches retirement age. Nonetheless, we have to take some systematic steps toward creating—if not security itself, then at least a sense of security.

Basic steps you can take toward satisfying the need to feel secure include a planned savings program for retirement, insurance to cover immediate needs should one or the other spouse die, and legally drawn wills. We were surprised at a fellowship supper with six other couples to find that three of those couples had not drawn up wills. Even if you feel you have few assets to will, you do need to draw a will with the aid of an attorney—if only to name custodians for your children and beneficiaries for any benefits which may accrue. And you will need to update your will from time to time, as your estate or family grows or as your children grow up and leave home. You may want to go a step further and have an attorney draw up a revocable living trust that includes much more than a simple will and doesn't have to go through probate court proceedings that are costly and delay the execution of your wishes.

4. *The need for leisure and relaxation.* "Any valid inventory of human needs must include the therapy of leisure." So reads an advertisement of a large corporation, with the added note, "Our leisure living communities, pleasure cruises, travel trailers, and motor homes are making life more enjoyable for many people." Ironically enough, the picture accompanying the ad shows a family out biking. Certainly recreation is a need, but it has been made expensive by our high tastes. It is time to remind ourselves that we can enjoy a lake without a boat. We can enjoy a boat without a motor. In some areas, we can ski without driving to the mountains. We can enjoy the winter out-of-doors without a snowmobile. And we can even go camping without a trailer or a motor home. Honest. We have done these things. And so have many others like us.

One summer we took a short camping trip with our family, our total gear being a nine-by-twelve-foot tent, a Coleman cookstove, and sleeping bags. At a lakeside campground, we found a quiet nook in which to pitch our tent, and then strolled down to the pleasant, shallow lake for an evening swim.

As we walked back, we found that we were going to have an opportunity to observe a contrasting camp style at very close range. Squeezed into the site next to ours was an enormous motor home. Our first greeting from the new arrivals was a marshmallow, underdone or overdone, tossed onto the road. We just managed to miss squishing it between our bare toes before composing our faces for a neighborly "Hello." We found the new neighbors friendly. Very. Perhaps their children had never been in something so quaint as a tent before, because they explored it thoroughly. *It's always fun to see how the natives live*, I thought to myself.

The marshmallow roast was still going on. "Want a marshmallow, little kid?" their children asked one of ours. Our children had never seen such big, puffy marshmallows. Ours were the smaller, less expensive variety. When our children offered to bring their own marshmallows and toast them at the fire, the others just laughed. "What do we need your marshmallows for, kid? We've got lots." The parents sat and chatted at the picnic table while Cam and I tried to do a bit of camp cooking. Were we going to fry our steaks in that little cooking pot? "Martha, go get our big skillet for these people." Was it getting a bit too dark for me to read? "Martha, get that big flashlight."

The party broke up early. "We've got to get an early start," the father explained. "We're going to do the mountains tomorrow." I thought about that as I crawled into our little tent. Do the mountains tomorrow! The Rockies? Should make a fairly full day! Except for the insistent barking of our neighbors' huge German shepherd, the quiet night beside the lake was undisturbed. Then, soon after six in the morning, the sound of a mighty motor filled the somnolent campground. The great engine fired, roared, then died. Again. And again. Inside our tent, the smell of raw gas was choking, and I was bidding a tearless "Adieu" each time the motor fired hopefully. Finally, the motor took hold, and after several long, throaty revs, our neighbors roared off. They were having a wonderful camping trip, they had told us.

More and more young families are seeking leisure and recreation in activities which are quiet, use muscles instead of motors, and — where possible — can be done "far from the maddening crowd." The beauty of it all is that many of these activities can be enjoyed at minimum cost. There never has been a price put on a sunset. Or moonrise. Or the quiet glow of a dying campfire beside a quiet lake. Or the high-pitched hum of that one last mosquito you failed to get out of the tent at zip-up time.

*   *   *

Our spiritual need of food and fellowship, our intellectual need to know and grow, our creative need to make and enjoy beautiful things, and our psychological need for security and "unwinding" through recreation are all needs known to our Heavenly Father. He is aware of our needs, as we should also be. Whatever our standard of living, He can help us to creatively design patterns by which we can meet these needs for ourselves and our families.

Chapter Ten

Putting Things in Place

It was just before Christmas. Cam and I were finishing up a bit of shopping at a large city mall. We had done a lot more looking than buying, with very little money in our pockets. As we stepped outside, I noticed an elegant woman drive up to the parcel delivery depot in a big white sedan. Her strawberry-blond hair was beautifully swirled, her makeup meticulous. I couldn't help but smile to myself at the obvious contrast between her economic condition and mine.

Then, as the young woman, wrapped in a luxurious fur, stepped out of the car to give directions to the boy carrying out her parcels, our eyes met, and we gasped with the shock of instant recognition.

"Peggy!"

"Maxine!"

She was a high school girlfriend with whom I had long since lost contact. We stood together on the sidewalk, chatting eagerly about the years that had intervened between high school and this moment. Peggy had done secretarial work in several large cities; then she had married a lawyer. "I'm so glad things have gone so well for you, Peggy," I told her.

"And how about you?" she asked. The physical realities of our situation were, at that moment, almost painfully apparent—I wearing a much-worn leather coat over a cotton dress and Cam in old jeans. "Well," I said, "we're trying to get started in farming, and our youngest child is just nine months old."

"Your youngest?" Peggy asked. "You have how many?"

"Four," I said. "Two girls and two boys. They're beautiful."

A shadow went across her eyes. "You lucky thing," she said. "We still don't have any. But we're hoping."

As she slipped back into her big, beautiful car, I waved good-bye and walked across the parking lot to our current second-hand car wondering which of two classmates was really the richer.

A friend of ours who also lost very heavily in the cattle business reversal that dumped us overboard told us, "My men keep asking me why I'm smiling. And I just have to tell them that if I'm healthy in body and relatively stable in mind—and if on top of that I have life in my spirit through faith in the Lord Jesus Christ—then, man! No matter how much money I may have lost, I am still a wealthy man!"

Defining "Poverty" and "Wealth"

What is poverty? What is wealth? No field could possibly be more relative than this. Today, of course, we are helped in our definition of poverty by the annual statement of government offices concerning the "poverty line." Radio announcers and newspaper writers grab up the releases from our economic councils. We read it; we hear it: "Any family of 3.7 with a net earning of less than $XY,000 per annum is living—officially—below the poverty line."

We did not know about the poverty line when we were kids. Looking back to our childhood, my brother once exclaimed, "We were poor, but we never knew it." Poor we may have been—poverty-stricken we were not. We had all the best of everything that really mattered. With good and godly parents, lovingly providing for far more than our physical needs while building a modest family home quite literally over our heads with their own hands, we children were anything but poor. Our personalities were sustained by love and encouragement; our minds stimulated by exposure to ideas, books, and interesting people; our spirits nurtured by the Bible, daily read and taught, and — more important — interpreted into life by our parents. When I go back to the city of Lethbridge and drive nostalgically down Twelfth Avenue South past the house where my earliest "little girl" memories took place, I am always surprised to see how small the house and yard are. By today's standards, our home was tiny. But to four growing children, it was home. We lived in the basement while our parents built the upstairs. And when the upstairs was completed and we "moved up," what joy! Our living area was doubled overnight. And we counted ourselves "kings of infinite space."

Today, it is much harder for families to keep the simple joy of not *feeling* poor. Having conducted a poll concerning attitudes toward poverty and riches, Martin Goldfarb in a *Reader's Digest* article concluded: "Poverty . . . is more than a physical thing; it's more than being deprived of dollars; it is an attitude, a sense of defeat, a loss of dignity."[1] For this very reason, government enunciations of the "poverty line" are misleading at best and, at worst, may be damaging. It is one thing to be poor. It is quite another to be told you are poor.

It is hard to work out a clear idea of relative poverty and relative wealth. Between the government telling us at what income we are poor or underprivileged, and the television presenting dramas on palatial show-home sets, it is hard to get a balanced idea of what real poverty or real wealth consists. Perhaps we have to turn to history, to read of the discomforts experienced by even the wealthy of two or three centuries ago, in order to understand the wealth we have in what we consider to be just ordinary, accepted comforts. Perhaps we have to come to terms with the housing conditions of the average peasant of the Middle Ages. Or really get an understanding of how the *average* person in many areas of our world lives today. Perhaps we need to go without a meal or two to find out what hunger really feels like. There are standards by which all of us, even the most pressed, are actually wealthy. There is a sense in which feeling "poor" or "rich" depends only upon to whose condition you compare your own.

There is, of course, such a thing as poverty. Real poverty. It is a miserable state of grinding necessity. When there is unremitting pressure in trying to make an income go around necessities — food, clothing, housing, and transportation — then there is, indeed, poverty. And poverty has its negative effect. It distorts the value of money. "More money" becomes very important. A person begins to dream of windfalls. And materialism becomes just as real a problem to the family which is truly experiencing poverty as it is to the very rich who also might be dominated by thoughts of material things. Or more so.

I remember how I gazed at those "Win a Dream Home" sweepstake advertisements that came our way — with chances to win (about one in ten million) based on buying anything from magazine subscriptions to face cream. Never had tickets for raffles had such drawing power; never before or since have I been so tempted to buy lottery tickets. In the end, we got our dream home — or at least a simplified version of it, in the way we were intended to: by praying and working and planning; by borrowing and repaying. But the experience of the power of *wish* during a time of deprivation gave me a deep sympathy for the many poor who become addicted to bingo and other games of chance; having lost hope in their ability to improve their circumstances, they cling to the hope of a windfall. I have also become deeply angry at governments that supplement tax revenue by lotteries. Because it is the poor who are most susceptible to the hope of a win, public lotteries amount to a form of taxation on the wistful hopes of the poor.

But physical, lack-of-money poverty is really only one aspect of the kind of impoverishment which cripples the human spirit and hampers the total growth of the individual. We need to develop discernment in a number of areas if we are ever to be released to enjoy the riches we may already have and are not recognizing as such.

First, to understand what state constitutes wealth and what constitutes poverty, we must distinguish between the temporal and the eternal. It is important for us as Christians to live in this present world in the light of the eternal one. The things of this life, no matter how good or how many, are only beloved trappings of a temporary earthly existence. Real riches must be spiritual riches, things which will outlast this earthly existence. This is what Jesus taught in Matthew 6:19-24; it is reiterated throughout the New Testament.

The physical is so immediate to us — as pressing as our own skins — and because it is proclaimed by so many forces which press physical and material needs and wants upon us, we may forget where our real interests lie. As believers in the resurrected Christ, who has pioneered the way into eternal life for us (see Heb. 6:19-20), we sense a reality beyond this life. The richest people in the world are those who are aware of the spiritual, eternal dimension of life into which we enter by faith. These people know that the real things are the things that cannot be seen with the eye.

Writing instructions to a junior devil on how to tempt a new Christian away from discipleship to Christ, "Screwtape" says:

> The sense of ownership in general is always to be encouraged. The humans are always putting up claims to ownership which sound equally funny in Heaven and in Hell and we must keep them doing so. . . . We produce this sense of ownership not only by pride but by confusion. We teach them not to notice the different sense of the possessive pronoun — the finely graded differences that run from "my boots" . . . to "my God."[2]

Let's face it: real poverty is the lot of every one of us — from those who work hard at wrapping inadequate incomes around the needs of a family to those who have so much that they are bored — if and when material things are first, and when this temporal world is treated as most important. Real poverty is the burning desire to possess, to claim more and more things as "mine." From this need to possess stems all sorts of contentions (see James 4:2-3). From this need to possess comes the continuous and much-encouraged breaking of the tenth commandment: "You shall not covet" (Exodus 20:17). From this need to possess comes our unending greed.

In a well-known essay on "The Blessedness of Possessing Nothing," Tozer describes the craving to possess as "a tough, fibrous root of fallen life whose nature is to possess, always to possess." He says:

> The way to deeper knowledge of God is through the lonely valley of soul poverty and abnegation of all things. The blessed ones who possess the Kingdom are they who have repudiated every external thing and have rooted from their hearts all sense of possessing. ... These blessed poor are no longer slaves to the tyranny of things.[3]

Another distinction we need to learn to make is between those things we need for physical survival in this temporal world and those things we merely crave in order to boost sagging egos, to confirm our identities somehow, or to project a success image. Joy Duncan, a writer friend of mine, commented in a letter to me:

> People ... suffer these days from a lack of identity. So many are caught in unrewarding jobs without the struggle and sense of direction our pioneers had simply to stay alive. It's a willy-nilly kind of existence. So they compensate by striving for *things* — "I know who I am now. I'm the owner of a new car." "Look at me. I'm somebody because the neighbors come to swim in my pool." It's a basic lack of self-worth that is alleviated by comparing oneself, favorably, with others — and, of course, if you can't compete in the "things" sweepstakes or don't measure up, it is devastating. It would be so simple if people would believe in themselves — which, as you point out, is a spiritual thing. If we are important to God, what else can matter?

We need too to distinguish between real faith in God and a mere faith in things. Turning Christianity into a "faith in God for things" is a sad, materialistic travesty of the Gospel which has rooted itself stubbornly in our consciousness.

A favorite hymn of mine says:

My goal is God Himself, not joy, nor peace,
Nor even blessing, but Himself, my God.[4]

But I still find the words easier to sing than really to live. Yet, finally, it is only as we get caught up in this larger vision—this possibility of intimacy with our Creator, a terrifying and purifying thought, that we can set down our preoccupying toys and direct our energies toward loving and knowing and bringing joy to the heart of the One "who loved me, and gave Himself for me" (Gal. 2:20).

Real poverty must be ultimately described in spiritual terms. It is to be "without hope and without God in the world" (Eph. 2:12). It was this kind of poverty that Jesus came to eradicate. Certainly He was concerned about physical needs. He fed the hungry. He healed the sick. And all without charge. He lived the simple life and shared all that He had and was with others. But over and over again, He pointed out that the deep need of the soul could never be satisfied with bread alone. It is as we recognize the inner emptiness of our spirits and come to Him that He meets our deepest needs. He fills our hunger with the living bread. He satisfies our thirst with the living water. He supplants our cravings for "things" with Himself.

Real poverty is to be without Christ. Or, having made a profession of salvation, not to find our existence saturated and blessed by His presence. Real poverty is to want things—anything—more than we want God. Real poverty is to have our lives cluttered, the good seed of God's Word "choked by life's worries, riches and pleasures" of this life and fail to bring any fruit to maturity (Luke 8:14).

Ultimately, we can conclude that real poverty is a state of mind in which *things* are uppermost. Real poverty is when hunger pangs force from my mind all thoughts but those of food. Real poverty is when the children are not dressed warm-ly enough for winter. Real poverty is when the housing we can afford is not adequate to the needs of our families. On the other hand, real poverty is—equally—when I have eaten so much that I am uncomfortable, and again, my thoughts center on food. Or when I have so many clothes that I have to spend a lot of mental energy making choices among them or finding ways to store them. Or when, regardless of my living condi-tions, I am discontent and brooding about how to have more. Real poverty is when material things are uppermost and press-ing—whether because we have too few or too many of them. It is poverty, because the human mind and spirit are made for higher things, worthier pursuits. As Barbara, a teenager in a girls' group I led, wrote:

> Like a bird, I soar
> Heavenward, My spirit free—
> Earth pulls me down.

When earth pulls us down, we are poor.

There is, however, a kind of poverty that Jesus called "blessed." He did not call it blessed to be cold or hungry or homeless (and everywhere in the New Testament, the writers take it for granted that as Christians we must do all we can to alleviate that kind of poverty). But Jesus called it blessed to be "poor in spirit" (Matt. 5:3). Actually, we are all poor in spirit. Spiritual poverty is our legacy. But Jesus calls us "happy" or "blessed" when we recognize our spiritual bankruptcy and turn to Him.

In the last book of the Bible, God's revelation given to John addressed to two different churches gives us insight into the real meaning of poverty and riches—not as seen from our own time-bound and thing-counting point of view, but from God's. To the church in Smyrna, the Spirit directs a kindly message: "I know your afflictions and your poverty—yet you are rich" (Rev. 2:9). Here, a church which was suffering persecution and physical poverty was warmly reminded of its real riches. Rich in the kingdom of heaven, where it really matters.

There is an entirely different tone in the message the Spirit directs to the church of Laodicea: "You say, 'I am rich . . . and do not need a thing.' But you do not realize that you are wretched, pitiful, poor, blind and naked" (Rev. 3:17-19). To be spiritually bankrupt and physically rich was the great problem of that church, and the tragedy of many of us who are believers today, especially in the affluent West. In that kind of poverty— that tragic, abject poverty which passes as wealth—there is no blessedness. To the poor-rich church at Smyrna, the Spirit says a word of encouragement: "Be faithful, even to the point of death, and I will give you the crown of life" (2:10). But to the rich-poor church in Laodicea, His word is admonishment: "I counsel you to buy from me gold refined in fire, so you can become rich" (3:18). Could it be that He was directing the church to ask for testing, for persecution, for adversity, in order to "melt down" the riches that the world can see in exchange for the true riches of having been faithful in testing?

These letters in Revelation summarize a tension that is felt in many of the epistles of the New Testament: the continual danger of mistaking "gain" for "godliness." Paul warns Timothy about "men of corrupt mind . . . who think that godliness is a means to financial gain." And then he spells it out: "But godliness with contentment is great gain" (1 Tim. 6:6).

Godliness—What Is It?

Godliness. What a strange, old-fashioned word that is, almost as remote as "holiness." We recognize it as a church word, a Bible word. But what does it look like in everyday clothes?

If "godliness" conjures images of long meetings with men preaching and women wearing buns, we probably need to consider what it really is: a life that is God-centered and growing toward God; a life in which the Holy Spirit is restoring the damaged and dented image of God so that in our priorities and attitudes and outlook we can be seen to be becoming more and more like the One who made—and remakes—us.

It consists, first of all, in having spiritual life, life that comes from God. We are born spiritually bankrupt, spiritually dead (Eph. 2:1). And only as we receive the vitality of the living Christ into our lives by faith can we experience what Jesus called the "new birth" (see John 3:1-18). Godliness begins with spiritual birth. But it does not stop there.

Godliness is seeing things as God does: The things of this world as good in that they add comfort to our short stay on this earth, but as secondary in importance to the ultimately real things which are spiritual and eternal; the things of this world as loaned only as a trust for which we will be called to give account. Godliness is using the good things of this life as God would, as a means of bringing blessing to others.

Paul outlined three reasons for diligence in business:

● To be able to pay our debts and live honestly (Eph. 4:28; 1 Thes. 4:11-12);
● To provide for ourselves and our own families (1 Thes. 4:11-12; 1 Tim. 5:8);
● To share with those who are less fortunate (Eph. 4:28). These are goals consistent with a godly attitude toward things.

If we really claim to be children of God through faith in Jesus Christ, then the first quest of our lives must be godliness. We can only develop godliness, or a godly perspective on things, as we deepen our devotional life, as we read the Word of God daily and soak up what the Bible reveals about ourselves and about our God. And we will always be challenged in our quest for godliness by that standard set by our Lord Jesus Himself: "Be perfect, therefore, even as your heavenly Father which is in heaven is perfect" (Matt. 5:48).

Whenever "things" become central in our lives, whether legitimate in themselves or not, then—if we are truly children of God—we can expect that His Holy Spirit will bring pressures to bear to move those things out of the center of our hearts and thoughts, out to the periphery where they belong. For the center of our beings must belong to God alone.

And then, going back to Paul's phrase describing "great gain," godliness is to be with contentment.

How to Find Contentment

Contentment is the key to the restful, rejoicing Christian life. Godliness first. And then, with God at the center of our lives, contentment follows. Things become only as important as they should be: necessary to sustain physical life, but not necessary to build up our egos or to maintain a special status. As we mature in our walk with our Lord, things should lose their luster and their appeal. Certainly, the more time we spend looking into the face of Jesus in devotional worship, the less interest the things of this world will hold for us.

In a recent phone call, my friend Donna told me, "Oh, Jerry thought about taking an extra job this winter, when the farming's a bit slack, so that we could finish up our basement. But I talked him out of it. You know, a few years ago that would have seemed mighty important to me. But now I know that the time we spend together as a family is far more important than wallboard on the rumpus room. It's funny how you get weaned from things, isn't it?"

I knew exactly what she meant. When we first thought we might be able to build a house, the idea consumed me. I spent hours making sketches, studying plans, scanning home magazines. And the Lord removed the possibility of building at that time. Later, with house plans again on the kitchen table, I found that I was interested only in making good and wise choices. The house had ceased to be a thing of importance in itself; it was now a means to the end of fulfilling our responsibilities to our growing children and of being settled so that we could serve the Lord effectively in the ministries He had entrusted to us.

* * *

When we know the basic provision of day-by-day needs, claiming by faith our daily bread; when we have healthy and secure children; and when we experience love and joy in our relationships with others, both within and outside of the home, then we are really rich. And when we live in relationship with God as our Father through faith in Christ, made real by the Holy Spirit, we are in fellowship with the whole awesome Trinity, and our wealth is beyond all reckoning.

The good life, as I see it, is the uncluttered life, the life in which the main goals are spiritual, the life in which the main riches are eternal. If along the way God should entrust to our care physical goods as well, then that is a responsibility just as much as a privilege. We need to be prodded into remembering that real security can never be found "in wealth, which is so uncertain," and so put [our] hope in God" (1 Tim. 6:17).

- Real poverty is to depend on things for identity or status.
- Real wealth is to find our true worth in the love of Jesus Christ.

- Real poverty is to depend on things for security or for happiness.
- Real wealth is to come to God for these things which only fellowship with Him can bring into our lives.

- Real poverty is to be thing-dominated in our daily lives.
- Real wealth is to have our lives centered on the Lord Jesus Christ.

- Real poverty is to make all the investments of our lives in material things.
- Real wealth is to make our primary investment in knowing God and serving others.

- Real poverty is to live in fear and insecurity in changing times.
- Real wealth is to know that, ultimately, our only security is God Himself and His promise of safe passage into His presence.

The good life is not one which can be defined as being above any arbitrary poverty line. It is, simply, "godliness with contentment." It is simplicity with dignity. It is having without holding. And that is — not only now, but ultimately — "great gain."

Chapter Eleven

Where We're at — and Where We're Going

Some years ago, I sat in the shade of the historical reconstruction of the fur-trading fort from which the city of Edmonton has grown and chatted with an historian, Dr. J.G. MacGregor, about conditions, past and present. A regional writer, he had himself lived through enormous changes here in western Canada. He spent his first winter in Canada in a tent, something which those of us who survive our bitter winters in warm houses find almost unimaginable. "Things will change back," he said. "It is inevitable. I don't think they will get as hard as they were for the early pioneers. But nowadays a young woman thinks nothing of going downtown and buying a new dress every other week. In the old days, it was an event to get new clothing once a year. And it will go back to that. I predict that before long the economy will be slowed down to that extent. And let's face it," he added thoughtfully, "it won't be all for the bad."

Those of us who read our Bibles know that Dr. MacGregor is no doubt right. Widespread economic chaos and famine are predicted in the Book of Revelation. Both are now upon our world. But surely this is not a time for Christians to go about with worried frowns, clutching frantically at our diminishing consumer power.

Looking Ahead

More recently, I talked with Dr. Bruce Wilkinson, a professor of international economics at the University of Alberta. He feels the outlook for the next two decades may be very grim, especially for a country like Canada with high international debt, but perhaps for other Western nations as well. Feeling that there will not be much relief from human suffering from governments which have already overspent, or from multinational corporations with little concern for the local populace, Dr. Wilkinson expects changes that will remind us that, biblically, the essential economic unit is the family. "Families will have to look after their own," he says. "And, furthermore, we will have to relearn how to interpret family not only in terms of our immediate kin, but in the larger sense of the church community."

Indicators already exist to show that income distribution both within individual Western economies and between nations is becoming less equitable with an increasing concentration of people at both ends: the highly wealthy and the desperately poor no longer buffered by a large middle class. Many futurists see this inequity as contributing not only to personal, but to global, insecurity. But, of course, attempts at redistribution may well lower the standard of living and eat into the security we have established for ourselves.

It is not, however, a time to wring our hands or to live in despair. Building a renewed sense of responsibility for each other into family and redeveloping a sense of local community—within the church and within a particular geographic locale—may be, finally, the best means of securing our futures. As we are obedient to God, we will rediscover what His people have always known: that ultimately, God—rather than our bank accounts or retirement plans or even our family or community—is our security. As we seek to live in obedience to Him, we can look to Him for His promised provision. Isaiah, speaking to a people of God in times of international instability, saw that God desired action, not just religious piety. Isaiah challenged them to consider that God's kind of "fast" or religious observance is:

To loose the chain of injustice
　　and untie the cords of the yoke,
to set the oppressed free
　　and break every yoke . . .
to share your food with the hungry
　　and to provide the poor wanderer with shelter —
when you see the naked, to clothe him,
　　and not to turn away from your own flesh and blood
(Isa. 58:6-7).

And when God's people obey, and live out principles of justice and compassion — at the family and community level as a starting point, but with an awareness of the larger international community as well, God's promise is clear:

Then your light will break forth like the dawn,
　　and your healing will quickly appear. . . .
Then you will call, and the Lord will answer;
　　you will cry for help, and He will say,
　　Here am I (58:8-9).

Despite seeing a pretty grim economic prospect, Dr. Wilkinson feels that Christians should not be living in fear. "We should praise God even at times of economic uncertainty because God is in control. We can live in peace, joyful that we can be alive at this time and that He has given us the privilege of having a little part in His great play."

The call to reconsideration of our lifestyle is being pressed upon us by a number of economic facts: recessions, inflation, the pressing needs of the Third World. It is a call which is being issued by politicians as well as preachers. It is a time, if not for sacrifice, at least for restraint. But it was our Lord Himself who issued a far wider call almost two millennia ago:

Do not store up for yourselves treasures on earth,
where moth and rust destroy, and where thieves break
in and steal. But store up for yourselves treasures in

heaven, . . . for where your treasure is, there will your heart be also. . . . You cannot serve God and riches (Matt. 6:19-21, 24).

A Glance Back

A few years ago the call for restraint was neither so pressing nor quite so inescapable. For the Christian young person growing up when I did, there seemed to be two main vocations or callings. One was to "full-time service," which meant limited income, but presumably adequate rewards in nonmaterial terms. The other equally honorable calling was to enter a career of your choice and, with any luck at all, to get rich. Not necessarily really wealthy, mind you. But by any global standard comparison, rich. The Christian press was turning out a spate of "success stories" for an eager, but not always perceptive, audience which gradually came to equate riches with righteousness, and financial acumen with faith. The super-successful businessman or professional person was promoted as the image of the *average*, or at least the *normal* Christian.

It all added up to a prevailing feeling that anyone who didn't "make it," on the same standard of success which the world around us used, was somehow a second-class citizen not only in society as a whole, but in the Church of Jesus Christ as well. The "gold-ring principle," whereby the "man . . . in goodly apparel" had obvious preferment within the church (see James 2:1-10), became an obvious feature of our evangelical churches.

Of course, this development can be given a broader historical setting. By doing so, we can help ourselves understand the assumptions on which we have built our value structures, structures which now, in the white light of the "present distress" seem to be so inadequate and so unscriptural.

First of all, there is the immediate historical context. My parents' generation lived through the Great Depression. The "dirty thirties" left an imprint on the mind of every person who passed through them, an ineradicable memory of pressing poverty which created a desire for things: not just for things in themselves, but for things as an indication of security. People who lived through those days wanted to be sure that they themselves would never know that kind of pressure again, and to be certain that their children would not have to go through such an experience of poverty. Making money, saving money, and buying things assumed an importance out of all proportion to needs in the shadow of the great want of the 1930s.

The same phenomenon has been seen in immigrants who came to North America in the wake of the European holocaust of World War II. In high school days, I had a friend who with her parents had lived in refugee camps after the war. She still spoke with a heavy accent, and even then her eyes had the haunted look of a child who had known hunger and cold and fear. I found her family, a Christian family, astonishing in its continuous talk and thought of "things." The accumulation of things seemed to obsess every waking hour for every family member. And, of course, with thrift and hard work, they were catching up quickly with their neighbors in material possessions. Such aggressive acquisitiveness cannot be criticized without a sympathetic understanding of its psychological basis.

A second fairly immediate historical aspect of our acceptance of wealth as a worthy goal in life lies in the history of the evangelical movement itself. This movement, and especially that part of it which in North America has been known as "fundamentalism," has been largely a movement of the poor and of the uneducated. And when any semi-outcast group begins to become socially acceptable, a very strong emphasis is placed on those things which bring upward mobility and respectability: education and wealth. Thus, in our conservative evangelical circles, we have in recent years tended to exalt those persons who are better educated and those who are more wealthy as the leaders who can bring us acceptance in our larger society.

These historical and sociological factors help us understand how the "company of the redeemed," named for a Man who had "no place to lay His head," has become a "company of the rich," (Matt. 8:20) or at least a company of people who look on riches as a seal of God's approval and as a worthwhile goal in life.

As we search out our roots deeper in history, we find that many major historians have seen links between the theology of the Protestant Reformation and the rise of capitalism. The Weber thesis, proposed soon after the turn of the century, has made a major impact on historical thought. Weber proposed that the "spirit of capitalism" had appeared in history as a result or by-product of the religious ethic of Calvinism.[1] R.H. Tawney's *Religion and the Rise of Capitalism* was both a refinement and a popularization of the Weber thesis. And while a causal link between Protestantism and capitalism is difficult to forge in a way that is utterly convincing, it has not been hard for scholars to see that the two movements, one spiritual and the other economic, have made good traveling companions. Many of the cause-effect historians who have followed in the Weber tradition have been hostile both to Protestantism and to capitalism, which certainly taints the objectivity of their work. But it is possible for us to learn from even hostile critics, and Tawney's biting comment is worth pondering:

> To countless generations of religious thinkers, the fundamental maxim of Christian social ethics had seemed to be expressed in the words of St. Paul to Timothy: "Having food and raiment, let us be therewith content. For the love of money is the root of all evil." Now [after the Reformation] . . . not sufficiency to the needs of daily life, but limitless increase and expansion, became the goal of the Christian's efforts. . . . Plunged in the cleansing waters of later Puritanism, the qualities which less enlightened ages had denounced as social vices emerged as economic virtues.[2]

The great Wesleyan revival of the eighteenth century is credited by historians as providing an all-important "brake for the un-trammelled self-interest of individuals pursuing the ends of their personal and private gain."[3] Yet John Wesley himself, as an old man, warned:

The Methodists in every place grow diligent and frugal; consequently, they increase in goods. Hence, they proportionably increase in pride, in anger, in the desire of the flesh, the desire of the eyes, and the pride of life. So, although the form of religion remains, the spirit is swiftly vanishing away.[4]

Reconsidering Our Values

It is important for us to understand on what foundations our traditions and assumptions rest. It is significant for us to discover just where we are at.

To those of us who grew up in the affluent post-war period in North America, the value of money was well taught. Christianity and the accumulation of capital seemed not only compatible, but causally linked together.

Now, however, we find ourselves living in a world for which we feel strangely unprepared. The goal of business success at any cost and the sometimes questionable profit-making no longer seem to be satisfactory as an expression of a Christian life view. We live in a world in which other goals and a broader ethic are required, not only for personal spiritual survival, but for national economic survival and for global physical survival. Business must thrive for people to have both work to do and income to make decisions about. But maximization of profit has to be balanced with ethical concern for the conditions in which people work and the impact of the process of production and the end-products themselves on the community and the environment.

More and more, people at all levels of our society are talking about a closed economy. While political leaders urge restraint, a bearded postal worker, involved against his own better judgment in a prolonged strike, says to a television interviewer: "Sure, I'd like to have more of the pie. But I guess we've all got to realize that there is only so much pie." The message is getting through. Only so much pie and the necessity of sharing it equitably: that is the greatest economic and social problem of our day. Only so much fuel, and how it should be apportioned.

Only so much air, and how it can be kept breathable.

The world economy, which became apparently endlessly capable of expansion through the discovery of half a world in the fifteenth and sixteenth centuries, and the industrial revolution of the eighteenth and nineteenth centuries, has suddenly snapped shut again. And we feel trapped in this closure. We find ourselves like the peasants in a medieval village, suddenly members of a vast "global village" in which many feel that we are, indeed, "our brothers' keepers." We know now that nonrenewable resources can be exhausted. We, as individuals and as nations, are aware that there is such a thing as debt becoming due and payable.

We sit in our living rooms and look into the "unseeing eye" of our television sets and see not just individuals but entire cities and nations going bankrupt. And at the same time we look into the empty eyes of swollen-bellied children of famine who are somehow, impossibly, still alive. And we know that somewhere, in some way, we are all personally responsible. But just sitting around with vague guilt feelings haunting us is hardly a sufficient response. We need to seriously reevaluate our whole set of life goals and to ask ourselves, "Where are we now? And where are we going?" We must put to ourselves the question: "Is my lifestyle supporting a famine somewhere in the world today?" We need to get back to our New Testaments to discover how truly Christian principles, enunciated by the Lord Jesus Himself and exemplified by the first-century Christians, can help lead the way in reaching out to others in our world.

If we are, indeed, not content to sit back and wait in helplessness for the waves of present and future shock to overwhelm us," we need to become actively involved in adjusting our goals, expanding our ethic, and moderating our lifestyle to meet the needs of this changing age. As believers in the Lord Jesus Christ, "we do not belong to the night or to the darkness. So then . . . let us be alert and self-controlled" (1 Thes. 5:6).

As we study the New Testament, we understand that one of the exciting things about the attempt to bring our lives back into line with the scriptural plumb line is that Christian principles are workable in any economic structure. The New Testament does not prescribe an economic system, nor does it endorse any particular economic theories. What it does do is tell the believer how to operate within whatever economic structure, or stricture, he finds himself. And how, in the light of biblical principles of justice and compassion, to critique and work for the improvement of the system in which we find ourselves.

Any cinching in of our belts that we undertake will not, in the long run, hurt any of us. It is very often only when we begin to feel pinched economically that we start to sort out the debris of our things-cluttered lives and decide which things are really important and which are peripheral.

Responding to Change

As citizens of a global village, a hungry global village, and as people who believe we will give account to our returning Lord for how we have lived, we must respond to the very obvious needs of others. Not just intuitively, sympathetically, or guiltily, but thoughtfully and philosophically, with a firm basis in the guidelines of the Scriptures, so that we can act boldly and with conviction and not merely react to things as they happen. We must, as those who bear the name of the compassionate Jesus, exercise leadership in finding better ways to share with others. We must take our cue from the Lord Jesus Christ Himself and get a correct valuation on the things of this world.

Many years have passed since Paul wrote this warning: "From now on those . . . who buy something [should live] as if it were not theirs to keep; those who use the things of the world, as if not engrossed in them. For this world in its present form is passing away" (1 Cor. 7:29-31).

If the time was short then, it is obviously far shorter now. As Christians, we dare not sit around, rendered helpless by "future shock." Instead, we need to be quick to adapt to the new economic and social realities of our world, quick to respond lovingly to the needs of others.

We live in urgent days, and our time of opportunity to share the Gospel, to share the good things of this world, may be very short. We need to live as people whose lives might be suddenly cut off. We need to learn, and we could learn from the Scriptures if we would come to them, the lessons that Aleksandr Solzhenitsyn learned through his experience of *The Gulag Archipelago:*

> What about the main thing in life, all its riddles? If you want, I'll spell it out for you right now. Do not pursue what is illusory—property and position: all that is gained at the expense of your nerves decade after decade, and is confiscated one fell night. Live with a steady superiority over life—don't be afraid of misfortune and do not yearn after happiness. . . . Our envy of others devours us most of all. Rub your eyes and purify your heart—and prize above all else in the world those who love you and wish you well.[5]

Seven years of Soviet prison camp and many more years of listening to the stories of hundreds of other prisoners taught Solzhenitsyn this truth, one which a child could learn from the Gospels, but one which we adults often tend to forget.

That the dark days detailed in the Book of Revelation are soon to break about this earth is all too clear. In an interview filmed before his death, historian Arnold Toynbee raised this question:

> Will man draw on the spiritual resources available from beyond himself—or not? On the answer to that question hinges the future of humanity—if there is to be one.[6]

It is no longer just the funny little man declaring, "The end is at hand." It's just that he knew it first.

So this is a time for uncluttered, tidied-up Christian living. Because the Lord is "patient . . . not wanting anyone to perish, but everyone to come to repentance" (2 Peter 3:9), there may yet be some time before the end. But events are inexorably bringing us closer to the return of Jesus Christ.

Living in Hope

If we do, indeed, live in the last days before the return of Jesus Christ, we are living close to the consummation of the great purifying hope of the church. Believers throughout the ages have lived in anticipation of the return of Jesus Christ, and the implication of the imminence of that return has always been to ask, "What kind of people ought [we] to be?" With the answer being: "You ought to live holy and godly lives as you look forward to the day of God and speed its coming" (2 Peter 3:11-12).

We can have the quiet confidence which Jesus intended to be the distinguishing mark of His disciples in the face of troubled times: We can obey His command to "lift up your heads, because your redemption is drawing near" (Luke 21:28) if, first of all, we are sure that we are His.

I remember once thinking about the return of my Lord and Savior, and being troubled by the thought: "When He comes, will I know Him? He is One whom I have loved, sight unseen. I have only artists' conceptions on which to base any visualization of the Lord Jesus Christ." And then the Lord brought to my mind the verse of Scripture, "He calls His own sheep by name and leads them out" (John 10:3). I realized, with a great sense of relief, that the important question was not so much, "Will I know Him?" but rather, "Will He know me?" For since I am one of His sheep, He will call me by name. What a restful confidence.

The Apostle Peter invites us to "be all the more eager to make your calling and election sure" (2 Peter 1:10), to take time to ascertain that we are, without doubt, participants in God's plan of redemption. And the Apostle John, in his first epistle, tells us the tests by which we can validate our personal positions relative to Jesus Christ. You may wish to study that letter in detail for yourself, but I see there these three main tests by which we can examine our claims to saving faith:

1. *The test of confession of sin (1 John 1:5-10).* If we try to lay claim to having done the best we could, or having lived as well as the next guy, as our basis for entering God's family, we "deceive ourselves." There is only one way in which we can know the cleansing that is necessary to make us acceptable in God's sight, and that is through confession and turning from sin. If we have confessed our sins and thus experienced forgiveness and cleansing, we have passed John's first test. If not, then this is the starting point. We can feel nothing but fear at the thought of Christ's return until we have cried out, "God have mercy on me, a sinner" (Luke 18:13).

2. *The test of obedience to our new Master (1 John 2:3-8).* Confession of sin is certainly the first step, but it is not the only one. John points out that we can know that we know Christ "if we obey His commandments" (v. 3). If we are changed persons because we live under new management, then we can face the visible, personal return of that Master, Jesus Christ, with confidence. Obedience to Christ will have two very distinct effects, as John points out:

• *Love (1 John 2:9-11).* Obedience to Christ as Lord and Master must result in an attitude of love toward our Christian brothers and sisters as well as toward those in the broader brotherhood of humanity (3:14-19). This kind of love has inescapable economic implications!

• *Right living (3:6-10).* Christ cannot be in control of a life without creating righteousness, or right living, in that individual. John is unsparing here. If we claim to have confessed our sins and thus to have entered into salvation, and then go on sinning, we're fooling only ourselves. As we abide in Christ and let His Holy Spirit give us power and direction for right living, we know "that when He appears we may be confident and unashamed before Him at His coming" (2:28). Not that we never again sin after our initial confession, but that we do not continue sinning: this is the important thought here.

Again, we need to ask ourselves: "Do our lives pass the test of obedience?" If not, perhaps we have never come to a point of decisively turning over our lives to the lordship of Jesus Christ. We need to reach the point where we cry out to the Lord as Saul did on the Damascus road (see Acts 9). When we do, because He is Lord, He will begin to bring our lives into conformity with His life. And we can look forward to His return with joyful confidence.

3. *The test of right doctrine concerning Jesus Christ (1 John 4:1-4).* John makes it very clear that what we think and say of Jesus Christ is very important. After Jesus' ascension, the angelic witness was that "this same Jesus" would return (Acts 1:11). We need to reexamine the scriptural evidence concerning the nature and person of Jesus Christ; we need to assure ourselves that we are, indeed, awaiting "this same Jesus." Not some nameless force for good, not some mysterious other manifestation, not just the kingdom of God on earth in demonstrations of love and peace among men, but "this same Jesus." The same Jesus who was born at Bethlehem, God in human flesh; who was heard and seen and known in Galilee, the Living Word; who was crucified outside of Jerusalem as the Lamb of God, the ultimate sacrifice for man's sin; who was raised from death, all His amazing claims fully vindicated in one act of enormous triumph. *This,* and no other, is the Jesus who will return in power. To be awaiting some other is to become vulnerable to the "false Christs" who, Jesus warned His disciples, would come before His own return.

Since God has ordained salvation only through His Son, Jesus Christ, right doctrine concerning Him is essential to any true experience of salvation—any experience that will pass the test.

Having set out these three crucial tests, John holds out this hope of perfect confidence to the believer: "I write these things . . . that you may *know* that you have eternal life" (1 John 5:13, emphasis mine).

We do not need to have our anticipation of Christ's return chilled by a tremor of fear if we have made sure of our relationship to Him. We can have further confidence as we look ahead if we know that our hearts are full of love for Jesus our

Lord, if we are learning to be untrammeled by affections and desires that bind us to this temporal world.

It is in the confidence of Christ's return that we face a threatening future. It is in the confidence that we are His that we embrace and declare this glad hope. And it is in the light of this that we affirm our position as "aliens and strangers on earth" (Heb. 11:13). Occupied with the day-to-day tasks of earning a living and making a home, concerned with the responsible conserving and sharing of this world's goods, we nonetheless live in the glad expectancy of His return: Maranatha! Come, O Lord!

Notes

CHAPTER 1: THE CALL TO MODEST LIVING
1. Francis Schaeffer, *Pollution and the Death of Man: the Christian View of Ecology* (Wheaton: Tyndale, 1972), 85.

CHAPTER 2: THE GOLDEN MEAN
1. Stanley Tam, *God Owns My Business* (Waco: Word, 1969), 112.
2. Harold J. Sutton, "Immortal Money: A Study of Tithing," *Alliance Witness,* 17 March 1965, 5.

CHAPTER 3: CONTENTMENT: LEARNED, NOT EARNED
1. David Grayson, *Adventures in Contentment* (New York: Grosset and Dunlap, 1906), 3.
2. Ibid., 5.

CHAPTER 4: LIVING ON LOVE
1. Catherine S. Chilman, Fred M. Cox, Elam W. Nunnally, *Employment and Economic Problems,* Families in Trouble Series, vol. 1 (Newbury Park: Sage, 1988) 46–48, 74–76.
2. Ibid., 46.

CHAPTER 5: STOPPING THE MERRY-GO-ROUND
1. Robert Schuller, *Move Ahead with Possibility Thinking* (Old Tappan: Revell, 1973), 107.
2. "A Way to Keep Your Debts Under Control," *Changing Times,* February 1969.

CHAPTER 6: BASIC NEEDS I: SHARING THE GOOD THINGS
1. C.S. Lewis, *Mere Christianity* (London: Fontana Books, 1970), 77–78.
2. Ronald J. Sider, "A Modest Proposal for Christian Giving in a Starving World: The Graduated Tithe," *Theology, News and Notes,* October 1975, 15.
3. John Wesley, *Works.* Cited by Kemper Fullerton, "Calvinism and Capitalism," in *Protestantism and Capitalism: The Weber Thesis and Its Critics,* ed. Robert W. Green (Boston: D.C. Heath, 1959).

CHAPTER 7: BASIC NEEDS II: FOOD AND CLOTHING
1. Doriz Janzen Longacre, *More-With-Less Cookbook* (Scottdale: Herald Press, 1976), 14.
2. Roland L. Weinsier, Sarah L. Morgan, and Virginia Gilbert Perrin, *Fundamentals of Clinical Nutrition* (St. Louis: Mosby, 1993), 7.
3. Weinsier et al., 4–5.
4. Longacre, 13.
5. Christie Harris and Moira Johnston, *Fig-Leafing through History* (New York: Atheneum, 1971).

CHAPTER 8: BASIC NEEDS III: A PLACE TO GO AND A WAY TO GET THERE
1. "Inside Out," *The Edmonton Journal,* 19 February 1994, E-1.
2. Ibid.

CHAPTER 9: THE OTHER NEEDS
1. A.W. Tozer, *I Talk Back to the Devil* (Harrisburg: Christian Publications, 1972), 29.
2. A.W. Tozer, *The Root of the Righteous* (Harrisburg: Christian Publications, 1955), 25.
3. Charles H. Spurgeon, *Faith's Checkbook* (Chicago: Moody, n.d.), 160.

CHAPTER 10: PUTTING THINGS IN PLACE
1. Martin Goldfarb, "Canada's Credo: Honesty Pays," *Reader's Digest*, June 1971, 30. For a different approach to the validity of official measurements of poverty, see Chilman, Cox and Nunnally, 107–108.
2. C.S. Lewis, *The Screwtape Letters* (London: Fontana Books, 1970), 109.
3. A.W. Tozer, *The Pursuit of God* (Harrisburg: Christian Publications, 1948), 21ff.
4. F. Green, "My Goal Is God," *Hymns of the Christian Life* (Harrisburg: Christian Publications, 1936), 351.

CHAPTER 11: WHERE WE ARE, AND WHERE WE'RE GOING
1. Robert W. Green, *Protestantism and Capitalism: The Weber Thesis and Its Critics* (Boston: D.C. Heath, 1959), vii.
2. R.H. Tawney, *Religion and the Rise of Capitalism*, New American Library (New York: Mentor Books, 1954), 206.
3. Marquis W. Childs and Douglass Cater, *Ethics in a Business Society*, New American Library (New York: Mentor Books, 1954), 55.
4. From John Wesley, *Works*. Cited by J.H. Plumb, *England in the Eighteenth Century*, Pelican History of England, vol. 7 (London: Penguin Books, 1963), 97.
5. Aleksandr I. Solzhenitsyn, *The Gulag Archipelago* (New York: Harper & Row, 1974), 591.
6. "The Prospects for Humanity." Interview with Arnold J. Toynbee, Canadian Broadcasting Corporation, October 27, 1975.

Printed in the United States
118205LV00002B/95/A